D1271050

COLOR MAGIC

ALSO BY CARLETON VARNEY

You and Your Apartment
The Family Decorates a Home
Carleton Varney's Book of Decorating Ideas
Carleton Varney Decorates Windows
Decorating with Color
Decorating for Fun
Carleton Varney Decorates from A to Z
Be Your Own Decorator
There's No Place Like Home
Down Home
Carleton Varney's ABCs of Decorating
Staying in Shape
Room-by-Room Decorating

COLOR MAGIC

CARLETON VARNEY

Illustrations by Ernest Fox

E. P. DUTTON, INC. | NEW YORK

Copyright © 1985 by Carleton Varney
All rights reserved. Printed in the U.S.A.

No part of this publication may be reproduced or transmitted
in any form or by any means, electronic or mechanical, including
photocopy, recording, or any information storage and retrieval
system now known or to be invented, without permission in writing
from the publisher, except by a reviewer who wishes to quote
brief passages in connection with a review written for inclusion
in a magazine, newspaper, or broadcast.

Published in the United States by
E. P. Dutton, Inc., 2 Park Avenue, New York, N.Y. 10016

Library of Congress Cataloging in Publication Data
Varney, Carleton.
  Color magic
Includes index.
1. Color in interior decoration. I. Title.
NK2115.5.C6V29 1985   747′.94   84–28706

ISBN 0–525–24348–8

Published simultaneously in Canada
by Fitzhenry and Whiteside, Toronto

DESIGNED BY MARK O'CONNOR

10 9 8 7 6 5 4 3 2 1
COBE

First Edition

For these friends

Neil Saunders
Amelia and Dan Musser
Lisa and Bob Kenna

and for
my special friends and associates too.

Elsie Lumsden
Ethel Connon
Norris Wakefield
Susan van Berg
Ernest Fox
Nancy Reeser

and for

my wife, Suzanne, and my sons,
Nicholas, Seamus, and Sebastian,
who have brought magic of all kinds
into my house

Contents

The Cast of Colors   *1*

Color Magic   *41*

Color Styles   *81*

Making Color Magic   *123*

How to Buy Color   *161*

INDEX   *173*

Color insert follows page   *86*

COLOR MAGIC

The Cast of Colors

In my twenty-five years of trying to determine people's color preferences, I have made many observations about the connections between color and personality. My observations have led me to believe that there is a blue-loving person, a red-loving person, a green-loving person, a yellow-loving person, and so on, and that these preferences also define people in terms of their other tastes and indeed their overall personalities.

Do you have a favorite color? Have you ever asked yourself that question? In order to use color magic in your own home you have to start somewhere, and that somewhere is in your head. If you don't know where your color preferences lie, you might find the color chart in the color insert helpful. What is interesting is that a lot of people within a color grouping share similar tastes and make similar choices. This is partly for cosmetic reasons. People tend to live with colors that enhance their skin and hair coloring just as they tend to wear those colors. Hence, because of their own appearance, people lean toward or away from the pink-toned, the blue-toned, or the yellow-toned colors. Other reasons for color preference can be found in the results of numerous color tests and surveys that have been administered by market and advertising researchers as well as color psychologists and experts in the field of interior design. What color or colors are you? To make color magic work for you, you have to look at that elementary question in a new way, with fresh eyes.

Red

Red is the color of desire, of sexuality, of impulse, and of blood. Red is a winning color. Red-loving people are active people rather than passive, sporting rather than sedentary.

They are people who like the competitive atmosphere, they like to lead, and they like to pursue their sensual appetites. The color red is the boldest choice of all. The red-loving person is electrifying, wishes to make dramatic kinds of statements, and is usually dark-haired or dark-eyed with skin that borders on tan. He or she loves to entertain and is a black-tie and restaurant-oriented person who feels good in a bright red lacquered dining room with a teak table, or a red dining room with a coffee-brown ceiling and rich, red Oriental rugs. The red lover likes an environmental mood that is showy, welcoming, and expressive. The red-loving person buys black dinner plates for that red dining room or a big zebra rug for the floor. He or she would paint the living room coffee brown, put a red sofa in front of the wall, hang a Venetian mirror over it, and accessorize with big brown tortoiseshell lamps and club chairs in bright red. He or she might do a bedroom with red corduroy on the walls. Red-loving people like brown and beige plaids, want the environment to be friendly yet dramatic, and like the feeling of cozy corners. But the red lover is also a person who likes heavy wood furniture, the Mediterranean look, and the black and gold French Empire style.

The red-loving man likes touches of metal, chrome, and brass. He likes pewter and a big barrel bar. He likes the image of the Knights of the Round Table just as the red-loving woman likes that of the Renaissance lady. Red-loving people tend to be cheerful. They mow their own lawns, have their money in blue-chip stock, have saved enough to be comfortable, and enjoy their life.

There are lots of primary reds to choose from: lipstick red, poppy red, fire-engine red, cardinal, strawberry and Chinese red, royal red, and geranium red are just some. These really-reds can add a lot of pizzazz to a room. Red lacquer walls are a great favorite these days. Black and white complement the vivid splash of a red wall nicely. You might try a black-and-white tweed rug with those lacquer red walls, or black and white tiles laid on the diagonal.

The use of red in home decorating scares a lot of people. Red doesn't have to take over a room, but it can relieve dreariness. Often people find themselves uncomfortable living in rooms without enough color to stimulate their eye. In such rooms, beige, brown, olive green, or rust might predominate. Think country garden reds in such a room and choose one of those vivid reds for the carpet. That addition alone will lift a boring room out of its doldrums. Or you might add bright red throw pillows, or change a rust-colored chair to a print of red, olive green, and brown on a white background. You could give draperies of a solid color like brown or beige a valance in a sparkling country floral print thus brightening up a window treatment without having to buy new draperies. Red wall-to-wall carpeting can be used to set off an Oriental rug to excellent advantage. Simply adding carnation-red pillows to an olive-green sofa will brighten up that sofa considerably. Use primary red in small doses and you'll be amazed how little is needed to brighten a room and change it from dull to cheerful. Like a strong spice, red can improve the flavor of a room as long as it doesn't take over completely.

Many people cover Mediterranean-style furniture in a red fabric such as scarlet crushed velvet. With such a sofa I would suggest using plenty of cool, juicy lime green, creamy white, and black. The walls could be white stucco, the carpet lime, and the draperies a heavy white linen with a black border, lined in scarlet, and hung on black rings from a wrought-iron pole. Then your large Mediterranean red couch would feel at home, blending with colors that complement it and cool it down rather than making it stand out and take over. Cool, fresh colors can balance hot, exciting red.

There's a type of red-loving person who wants a red kitchen. This person is usually somebody who wants the kitchen to have a lively quality about it that is inviting. I've noticed in my career that women who have red kitchens spend a lot of time there cooking or having friends in to chat. They like to have a breakfast table and stools, a small desk, and a cookbook section. There are usually a lot of appointments and accessories around this person's kitchen, which is definitely not the clinical, Joan Crawford-style kitchen, where everything was stainless steel and white, and the food the only color interest.

If you are the kind of person who is attracted to a busy, lively conversation-filled kitchen, you might like to try doing yours in red. I would pick bleached wood cabinets or cabinets of snow-white laminate. For countertops I would pick a bright cherry red. However, a lot of people don't like countertops of anything but wood. The red-loving kitchen person usually has a chopping block set in her countertop. On her walls she might use a wallpaper of bright red strawberries with white and yellow strawberry buds and an apple green and orange stripe. For the windows, she might pick a coordinating fabric. The red person would have a breakfast table of pine. There would be a certain down-home quality about this room combined with a modern feeling. Old-fashioned, stripped-pine captains' chairs with arms would be the kind of chair the red-loving kitchen person would select, and she might make seat cushions for them of a green and white geometric pattern and tie them onto the chairs with bows. She would have red placemats and china designed with a strawberry motif. That design wouldn't have to coordinate absolutely with the wallpaper, but it would still feature strawberries. There might also be a lot of strawberry collectibles on the walls and shelves so that people always would know what to give this red-loving hostess for a little gift. There would be a copper light fixture in the kitchen with a scalloped copper shade. Red lovers would also have copper kettles and pans about, as well as hobnail candle holders on the table at night, and red glasses. Water would be poured from a strawberry-colored glass pitcher.

Blue

Blue, in all its many hues, elicits a deep response of tranquillity, permanence, and unity. Blue is the color of the ocean in its untroubled state and of the sky free of turbulent weather. Blue satisfies a great human need for a peaceful atmosphere.

Blue-loving people are usually quiet. They are sometimes on the cool side. Blue-loving people are orderly. When you think of the term *shipshape,* for instance, you think of blue. Rarely do yacht owners want anything but blue and white in the interiors, especially when they have mahogany woodwork. The presidential yacht, *Sequoia,* was one of my recent projects, and it has a wonderful mahogany patina. When I did the interior of the *Sequoia,* I chose a blue that had some green in it as opposed to the more popular skipper blue. I felt that blue green with mahogany walls was appropriate to the boat's period. Those early yachts were rarely furnished in skipper or navy blue but in a watered blue green. I put a blue-green carpet in the big salon. It had a border of beige and brown to match the color of the walls. I used blue-green damask on the dining-room chairs and for the draperies. I felt that there was a serenity to the ship that a navy or skipper blue or primary paint-box blue would not have enhanced. Those colors would have been too sharp a contrast to the subtle patina of all that beautiful aged wood.

The blue person can be either blond or dark-haired with blue eyes, but rarely has green eyes. The primary blue person has a yellow-toned complexion, because a pink-toned skin color does not work well with strong blue. The ruddy-faced person would be more likely to pick a pastel blue. On the whole, light pink is not a color to use with primary blue unless it's used very carefully.

Modern blue-loving people like chrome, Lucite, and tartans. They will use a navy-blue wall with a tartan plaid in black, blue, and beige. A more traditional blue-loving person will like Chinese tea canister lamps and opaque shades. The modern blue person will use white lampshades so that everything sparkles. Traditional blue-loving people who favor the Continental style will prefer opaque or even dark shades. However, everything in their environment will gleam, especially the wood surfaces.

Blue-loving people love baskets. They will never use vermeil on the table, but choose silver. They will set a table with a lot of glass. For example, for serving a salad, a blue-loving person would choose a big clear glass bowl, clear glass plates, and white placemats. A blue person likes watery blue glasses with rims of gold.

Blue people do not like tablecloths but prefer the exposed wood, so that you can see the cleanliness of the wood itself. They don't like to cover up things. The blue person likes low candles. Those who prefer the Continental style like silver sconces against a navy-blue wall. Blue-loving people might have a royal-blue carpeted drawing room and they might use mustard-colored velvet as an accent. Blue persons love Chinese exportware in blue and white.

In the bedroom, blue-loving people who want a modern look might choose a blue carpet with mustard gold walls and white trim, or they might choose silver walls.

Here is a bathroom for the person who loves skipper blue. All the tiles and the fixtures in the bathroom would be white. You could paint the ceiling paint-box blue. For the walls, you could use a blue and white geometric on a silver background. You could add blue-and-white towels and blue tile on the floor. At the windows, you could go clean and modern with white louvered shutters or chrome venetian blinds that do not rust. White powder bottles with mercury silver tops and a clear shower curtain on a chrome rod would be attractive accessories. A caveat about this blue room: if anything is out of place it will show. When you use bright blue, you have to keep everything very crisp and orderly.

Blue may be the all-time favorite decorating color, but it is rarely primary blue, which most people find too strong and bright. People choose weaker versions of blue such as sky blue, Wedgwood, peacock, turquoise blue, steel blue, or robin's-egg blue, but almost never the strong blue that is unmixed with green or whited down to a pastel. However, royal and navy blue are strong decorating color choices. Try using primary blue with pale green and chocolate, emerald green, persimmon, and lots of white. Think of the way nature uses blue—mixed with lots of shades of country greens and browns. Then primary blue becomes fresh and delightful and easy to use.

I can imagine an Oriental rug used as the basis for a primary blue room to great success. The rug might have a background color of soft teal green with figures of rose, deep blue, pale blue, gold, and tan. Rather than paint the walls a bright blue, which most people would find too much blue to live with, I would paint them a pale champagne shade instead, with gleaming white woodwork and a white ceiling. The sofa could be covered in a bright primary blue with white trim and the club chairs in a stripe of bright and pale blue on a champagne-beige background. Sofa pillows of pale pink, bright pink, and sea green could provide accents. Draperies could be in pale blue, with white trim like the sofa, and lined in bright blue. Paintings and accessories could feature bright blue, pale green, golds, and bright yellows.

If you feel that there's too much blue in a room you are planning to do over, try combining it with yellow—not bright yellow, which would not provide enough contrast to bright blue, but a pale lemon yellow. If your too-blue room is a living room, you might paint the walls in the pale lemon shade with white woodwork and trim, keep the blue rug and the draperies, and cover the couch in an ice blue and white floral pattern. You could then use a yellow and white stripe for pull-up chairs.

Yellow

The yellow person is generally a delight. Of all the primaries, yellow is the most airy and cheerful, and that describes the yellow-loving person: one who looks for sunshine even when there isn't any. A yellow-loving person might do a dining room with yellow moiré walls and yellow draperies trimmed in white. She might choose a French chair in a light fruitwood and upholster it in a yellow and gold cut velvet. Yellow-loving people like an all-white tablecloth and a semiformal pattern to the china; they might choose a plate with a small border of gold or a field flower of morning glory blue.

Yellow can provide an immediate lift in a house, particularly in northern rooms. Exposure has a big effect on color. If you have a northern room, yellow can fill that room with sunshine. Consider yellow walls, white trim, and a yellow-painted ceiling and you will have a sunshine glow all day long.

The yellow person likes to combine gray and white with yellow. A yellow-loving woman might have in her bedroom a yellow ceiling but gray-on-gray damask walls and a gray carpet. Her headboard might also be gray, and she might use softly tinted yellow sheets. She might use yellow opaline lamps with gold bases and gold trim and white silk shades trimmed in yellow. In that gray room she might have a chaise longue covered in yellow silk with accents of white and gray pillows, or she might use furniture that's Venetian in feeling, painted gray with a delicate floral design. She might use a big Venetian mirror in the room and a chest with a bombé front.

The yellow person will combine yellow with a soft, bittersweet pink and green. This combination can provide a Southampton, Long Island, look—flowery and sunny.

Yellow-loving people like crystal, especially boxes that have bronze doré tops. If they are drawn to the Continental style, they like rock-crystal candlesticks with bronze doré bobèche holders, which go well with Aubusson rugs, another favorite choice of lovers of yellow. They like dining-room tables with marquetry-bordered tops and bases painted white with gold trim. They generally like French furniture, if not provincial, then period French. They like kidney-shaped sofas with skirts on the base that have inset pleats in soft yellow. They like tufted curved-back sofas and French-paneled walls. They like Chinese decor if it is light in feeling. They like porcelains and demilune console tables painted white. They like chintzes in bedrooms, valances at the windows with ruffled borders, and curtains lined with pink and white chintz. They are much more pastel-oriented than blue people. They like yellow and white bathrooms with white marble countertops. They like their towels white with a pink monogram, and shower doors as opposed to shower rods.

The true yellow-loving person has an open heart and serves light fare in food and drink. They like a twist of lemon in the glass. In fact, they love lemons, and will even have a bowl on the coffee table filled with lemons and limes. Yellow-loving women tend to dress in light colors. In summer they wear white. They love full-skirted round tables and appliquéd white linen or cotton tablecloths, but not lace.

The yellow-loving man is one who likes to do things right. He wears a blue-and-white-striped suit and a yellow button-down shirt. On weekends he wears white or navy pants, generally unbelted, and an open-collar pink shirt with a soft narrow blue stripe. His wristwatch will never have a platinum band, as he prefers the warmer metals such as gold.

For accents yellow-loving persons like pink, soft Delft

blue, and lettuce green. They generally don't like navy or red, as these colors are too strong and overstated for them. If they do anything in red, it probably would be a cinnabar shade. For instance, they might choose a cinnabar-red rice bowl with a black top to fill with fortune cookies for a party.

Yellow is a brighter color than red but less dense and heavy. Yellow likes to radiate like the sun. It also stimulates the body's nervous system, but less so than red. It suggests lightness and cheer, and although it makes a strong statement, it does not provoke as much as red does. Yellow is a color that loosens up tension, whereas green concentrates it, which is why they must be used together carefully so they don't cancel out each other's properties. Yellow is a volatile color in that it is never at rest. It is always busy radiating and reflecting and expanding. Like the sun, it has a powerful effect on other colors. Yellow can create a halo effect around other colors and actually change their nature when used next to them. Whereas green is the color of stability, yellow is the color of change. It is forever altering the properties of light in a room.

For an indoor/outdoor dining room in a warm climate I might use primary yellow right out of the can. I would paint all the walls this bright yellow, or I would use a trellis-patterned wallpaper with a bright yellow background. There are many trellis patterns on the market, particularly in yellow, white on yellow, and yellow on white. I would install this same pattern on the ceiling to give the feeling of an outdoor gazebo. For a carpet I would use a more practical color than yellow such as a Florida lettuce or a citrus green. From the ceiling I would hang a fly fan with natural-wood-stained blades and a ball light. These fixtures are easily available and come packaged ready to install.

For furniture in this sunny room I would prefer wicker, new or old, painted white. It might be upholstered in primary yellow or in a yellow and white stripe or in a pattern with palm fronds and flowers on a white background. Or you might use a yellow with a small geometric pattern in the same colors, although I would prefer the frond design. I would also use big-backed, white wicker fan chairs with a 1940s look. Or you might choose another popular forties look, bamboo, also painted white. On these chairs I would have a yellow-and-white cotton tweed, which is soft and durable.

I see the dining table as wrought iron painted white with a glass top on which the hostess could set a white basket full of lemons. There could also be straw placemats of lettuce or citrus green to match the color of the carpet. You could choose Italian dinnerware in a yellow-and-white sunflower pattern. The room could also be filled with hanging white pots filled with ferns. There could even be a sunshine yellow hibiscus plant in a big white pot sitting in the corner. This use of primary yellow and white gives you the feeling of being on a Caribbean island.

Green

Over the years, I have found that secondary-color lovers are more complicated than primary people. When we come to secondary colors, the major secondary color to me is the combination of blue and yellow, which, of course, makes green. Green is a soothing color. It is a more earthbound color than blue, more assertive, and more tangible. It doesn't radiate like yellow, although yellow gives green its brightness. Green is the color preferred by people who like to accumulate possessions and who like constancy and solidity. What could be more constant, assertive, and solidly "there" than a towering green deep-rooted tree? A green room with dark green walls and a green carpet is a strong room. The walls could be covered in felt, or suede, or painted. Living in a predominantly green room is almost like living in a kind of peaceful forest. The feeling of green is one of strength, serenity, and enclosure. The person who likes a green room is generally a nature person. He or she likes wood, stone, slate, and brass. There's a special magic about brass against green. Stainless steel and green, on the other hand, never really work for me. Stainless turns green into something cold. Even colder to me than a green-and-stainless-steel room is a green-gray-and-chrome room. That's icebox-time to me. But a room that has green walls, wood beams, wood shutters in the windows, and a beautiful log-cabin red quilt thrown against the sofa is a warm and lively room.

Green and red rooms are a lot like Christmas packages to me, but they were a favorite of my predecessor, Dorothy Draper. I remember Mrs. Draper taking part in a lecture series where she would come on the stage and present two packages. One was wrapped in green-and-white-striped paper and tied with red ribbons and bows with flowered centers. The other was tied in brown paper with twine. She would hold out these two packages to the audience and ask, "Which of these two packages would you want?" and of course her audience would always clamor for the Christmas present. Maybe in these days of high-tech living a lot of people would go for the brown paper, but in Dorothy Draper's heyday they all clamored for rooms wrapped like presents.

I like Christmas green with a rich, deep rust. I should like to see walls painted dark green as a background for a dark green sofa. In this room I would use a rust, green, and white print in accent pillows and a green carpet. I would use brass rods at the windows and many beautiful tones of wood. I might feature Victorian-Western in such a room with a rolltop desk and student lamps with green billiard shades.

Green-loving people like leather and horn cups and rocking chairs of wood painted green, particularly on front porches on a painted gray floor. A green person likes a room that encompasses. A green person is a reader and is outgoing but only at specific times. The green person has the ability to be at home almost anywhere, like green itself.

Most people make the mistake of watering green down too much. They mix it with too much yellow and get avocado or they make it too blue turning it to turquoise. I believe green is the hardest decorating color there is, and as evidence I can cite the problem so many people have with avocado.

I've been writing my syndicated newspaper column "Your Family Decorator" since the 1960s. The column receives a multitude of letters and most of these are from people who want to know how to use color in their homes. The most frequent questions are similar to this: "I have beige walls, my rug is avocado, I have a beige sofa and an orange chair. What can I do?" Or "I have a bedroom with beige walls and an avocado carpet. What can I do with bedclothes, curtains, and slipcovers?" Over the years I have discovered that the most popular color in rugs, particularly wall-to-wall carpets, is avocado. As I travel around the country on lecture tours, I make bets with myself that in whatever home I visit the rug is going to be avocado. The favorite color scheme built around avocado is beige and rust with a dash of orange. I would say that is how 78 to 80 percent of America lives. Unfortunately, there's nothing primary or secondary about the color of avocado. It's a green that isn't grass, emerald, or hunter, but a grayed-down yellow green that has neither zip nor zap.

What does one do with those beige walls, avocado sofa or rug, and orange chair? How does one go about making color changes without selling or throwing out the sofa or rug? Sometimes I recommend that people do buy new furniture or a new carpet, but I try to remember that some of those first decorating mistakes people make, particularly in carpet, cost a great deal of money. Carpet is the biggest expense in decorating, and avocado is still the most popular color. So, I usually say keep the rug and the sofa. Paint the room a soft yellow and buy for the windows an English-style floral print fabric of avocado, pink, orange, leaf green, and sky blue with a yellow background. Re-cover the pair of orange chairs in that same fabric and outline-quilt the print to give a little bit of sparkle to the room. Accent the avocado sofa with pillows of light blue and pink.

I often suggest for a little girl's room with an avocado carpet that pink will redeem the avocado in a pretty way. In a boy's room with an avocado rug, try chocolate-brown walls. You can use a plaid of dark brown, beige, bright green, and avocado in the curtains or bedcovers. The way to make avocado and beige sing is with an infusion of color.

If one were to paint a whole house avocado I believe it would be the most dreary place imaginable. Avocado is a tone of green that's even darker than those institutional-green classrooms I sat in as a child. Avocado also reflects badly on complexions. It's one of the colors never used, for instance, in a hospital nursery. It makes a baby's skin look puce green. But avocado seems to be one of those colors that people feel "safe" with. Color *is* something that frightens people, and most people don't like change. If there's a change in their environment, they feel very unsettled.

If you've been living in a "safe" avocado room and are tired of it, you probably don't have to change it completely, just give it a lift. There are lots of colors that can be used with avocado to give it sparkle. One of the color combinations I like to use to cheer up avocado is Chinese red and hot mustard with black-and-gold accents. If you have an avocado rug, paint your walls a bright Chinese red. On the sofa use a print of bright red flowers with avocado leaves on a beige background with a touch of sky blue in the floral pattern. Put beige pillows with a red or avocado border on the sofa. Cover one chair in plain beige and bring in a postmodern-style black lacquer coffee table with gold trim. I would use big shiny brass lamps against the red wall with white silk or linen shades.

One of the things that "dead" colors like avocado need is jewelry. By jewelry I mean metal objects like lamps that can be brass, silver, or copper, the latter being a big favorite with people who like avocado schemes. But stay away from white or dull-colored stainless steel, which turns green cold.

Fall colors are popular in American homes, but rarely are they used successfully. Here's an example of a rust and avocado scheme in fall colors that really works. Paint your walls a beautiful rust, but one that has a sparkle to it. Paint the trim beige white. Your sofa might also be rust. On the floor I would use a plaid carpet of avocado, brown, black, and beige and I would accent the rust walls with big Southwestern clay or crockery lamps with linen shades. You might use a coffee table wrapped in linen or a sunflower-yellow lacquered coffee table that would add a new bright accent to the room.

A pair of chairs or camel-seat ottomans could be covered in beige suede. A big Southwestern picture or a woven wall hanging or tapestry would make a handsome accent, especially in glistening colors of rust, yellow, avocado, and bright red.

If the room had a fireplace, big brass andirons and a cactus plant in a big brass pot twenty inches or more in diameter would look good in it. Baskets also look good in a fall-oriented room.

I much prefer my greens in the green-blue range than the yellow-toned avocado range, but this cooler green is not an easy color either. For instance, take a deep blue green. Is the shade green blue? Or blue green? It's interesting that blue green became the word for the color because it was a green that had been blued, never a blue that had been greened. There's a fine line between blue green and green blue. To work successfully, the intensity of the green needs to be stronger than the intensity of the blue.

When you do a blue and green room, which is a popular choice these days, you need to find shades whose intensities don't fight with each other. For instance, you might paint the walls blue green and use a beige carpet. A fabric of blue-green background with rose, light green, a dash of light blue, and pink in the pattern could cover the sofa. At the windows you could use the same print as on the sofa, but lined in a pink and rose taffeta plaid. For carpeting I would choose a rosy-pink color. I would use a large-scale light fixture such as a big chandelier to give those blue-green walls enough light to stand out at night. The blue-green room also needs lots of wall lights. They could be sconces with pretty shades used with large mirrors to reflect a fire in the fireplace. Blue green needs jewelry, like mercuried ashtrays or several mercuried vases that could sit on the mantelpiece or a Victorian needlepoint panel of several roses in pinks and greens framed in a gold leaf and hung above the mantel. Blue green needs portraits, placemats with crocheted borders, and crystal glassware.

Another current favorite of the green-loving person is grass green, the favorite color in Southampton and Palm Beach. Grass green is an English color often called green-apple green. It's often used in wallpaper and may feature borders with swags containing pretty arrangements of roses and daisies. When the English do a green wall, they do it much better than we Americans do. Americans tend to make grass-green walls too shocking and bright. I often see a too-grass-green carpet, generally in a shag, used with a big white wicker sofa covered in a chintz print with every color imaginable: yellows, pinks, blues, oranges, lavenders, peacock blues, hydrangea blues, you name it. These colors work in the bright light of day when the sunlight is intense enough to wash out the brightness of the green. However, where there isn't that kind of intensity of sun-washed light, bright green is a difficult color to use properly.

Celadon is a soft shade of green that doesn't require so much light. It is a particular favorite in what I call Continental interiors as well as being quite appropriate for a Williamsburg-style room. A person who likes a celadon room likes quietude and to feel that life should not be filled with too many surprises. For a Williamsburg room I would paint the trim a soft ecru beige and the walls in a very soft celadon green. At the windows I would have a print on a beige background featuring celadon, lavender, light melon, and pink with birds and vines among the flowers and leaves. I would cover the sofa in a celadon-colored fabric similar to the wall color and add pillows of melon and beige and some handsome antique needlepoint pillows with a beige background. I would cover a wing chair in the room to match the floral print drapery. I would use a butler's tray as the coffee table and a pair of rectangular drop-leaf Pembroke tables with one rounded side extended, so that they looked like half ovals on either side of the sofa. Over the sofa I would hang a family portrait tied to the wall with a white silk bow. The lamps could be Chinese porcelain with a melon design on a white background and white silk shades.

Such a formal-style room would often have a grand piano and a fireplace. Above the fireplace could be a grouping of bird or botanical prints, perhaps from an old book. I would have brasses in front of the fireplace and in the summer would fill the fireplace with rhododendron leaves.

Purple

Purple is the most mystical of all colors. It combines the vastly different properties of red and blue, one excitable, the other calming. Consequently, the qualities of purple are bound to be rather complex. Medical findings say that purple is the color that visually predominates while someone is under the influence of psychedelic drugs. It is intimate, even erotic, which may be why it is such a popular bedroom color.

Interesting tests have been conducted regarding people's reaction to purple. People who were judged to be emotionally or mentally immature preferred purple to other colors. Preadolescent children were found to be fond of violet to an amazing degree.

Purple is also identified with things regal. Two colors the English like most of all are both royal colors: bright red and royal purple. I think that the popularity of these two colors relates to the fact that the king and queen of England identify themselves with them. In the Barclay Hotel in London, you will find that the color scheme is red and purple. The restaurant is purple and lavender. The lobby is purple. Purple is the color of England to me, from royal to heather.

My predecessor, Dorothy Draper, used a Baroque approach to purple in her apartment, which had one of the most interesting living rooms I've ever seen. There, Mrs. Draper took purple and red to the "max," you might say. The walls were painted aubergine, or eggplant, the darkest shade of purple. The ceilings were painted white as were all the crown moldings and lintels, which were white semigloss enamel. At the entrance to the living room was a double door of polished mahogany. At the windows was a damask pattern of beige on white with white undercurtains. Against these beige damask draperies was a sofa covered in peacock satin. Accenting the sofa were bright-red velvet pillows. The floor was a deep, dark, rich mahogany on which lay white bearskin rugs. In front of the fireplace were four swivel chairs covered in red velvet.

On either side of the sofa were a pair of chairs covered in a chintz of bright red, purple, white, and sky blue. They were pulled up to a mirrored coffee table. There was also a Venetian breakfront that held wonderful porcelains and there were card-table chairs in black and gold with cane backs around a mahogany card table, where she would sometimes have lunch with her friends. It was a remarkable looking room and the deep purple walls made it look rich and gleaming.

Purple has a great appeal to the older generation. When I grew up, I always thought of purple in relation to my grand-mother. It's an "old" color. Something about it appeals to older folk a lot, maybe because it's steeped in centuries of ecclesiastical tradition and is soothing. I did Ethel Merman's bedroom many times over the years. As the years went by that room went from loud and bright to cool, calm lavender and purple. I believe the color was very comforting to her. The room had white walls and a brass bed that she had had for many years. Her skirted table was done in a fabric called "Old Lace," a white lace pattern with white gardenias on a background of lavender. She used the same fabric in her curtains and chairs. The ceiling had a lavender tint to it, and the carpet was deep green.

When I've been involved with older couples, I've found that they usually like tones in the purple family: violet, laven-der, orchid, lilac, mauve, and wine. Fortunately these are easy colors to work with. You can use lilac with apple green and white, or wine with white or white and pink, or lilac with white and sky blue, or violet with white and red, or orchid with white and rich coffee, or mauve with white and peach, or lavender with white and royal blue. Unlike orange, which gets along with very few colors except as an accent, purple gets along with just about any other color as long as you introduce a shade of white.

When it comes to lavender for the older set, you can't use the grayed-out postmodern shades so popular today. Colors for the elderly have to possess clarity and light. Whereas the postmodern purple is what I call a no-color, being neither this nor that when held up to nature, the purples for the older set must be natural, as natural as the violet and the rhododendron.

I often do rooms for older couples with walls of lavender, a sky-blue ceiling, and prints of what I call Bonwit-Teller violet, vine green, and white. There are many sheet patterns available in that combination, which appeal more to older people than to young people.

There is a freshness and at the same time an old-fashioned quality to the lavender flower. I have noticed a lot of fabric prints of late featuring lavender and white lilac blossoms on a green or even black background. The lilac has been popular for so long that it can seem nostalgic. The lilac is not a flower that has been genetically altered or changed in any way, which makes the lilac bush one of those reliable perennials. Times may change, but lilacs bloom every year. Lilacs come in luscious shades that have a different fragrance depending on the color, as lilac lovers will tell you. There's the ever-popular lavender lilac and the deep purple Persian lilac. There is also a delicate raspberry shade of lilac and a cream-to-ecru white lilac. I believe that the aroma of lilac is part of the attraction of purple.

Hermione Gingold was another lady I worked with who favored lilac. Her apartment was full of white wicker, lace, lilac, and white. Lavender and ecru lace is a hard combination to resist. It goes wonderfully with old wood. Lilac people, many of whom are charming eccentrics, feel most people laugh at them for loving lilac, because when they go lilac they all but plant a few bushes in their room.

Postmodern purple is all the rage these days. This grayed-out lavender often is used together with a dusty-rose beige and an aqua gray to complement the Art Deco–style furnishings so popular in the postmodern room. It is not unusual to enter a very modern apartment in Boston or St. Louis and find the young inhabitants there living in a room of purple gray with white trim. The carpet might be stripes of purple gray and white and the sofa a burgundy tone with accents of what I call airport raspberry. Airport-lounge colors are often postmodern, as are those used in the most chic of the spas. However, in my mind, magenta against purple gray is forever associated with airlines. The good thing about these intense colors is that they instantly fill up a big space.

One of the most effective color combinations in the post-modern range is lilac, white, and green. It's one of the combinations that is becoming more and more popular among younger people. I just did a house in Greenwich, Connecticut, for a young couple in which the living room was painted a blue lavender close to mauve. It had warmth to it, but also a definite modernity.

I think of the modern lavender person as someone who likes a modern bar in the living room, and a big stereo set, and lots of slinky sofas. Dhurrie rugs are great for purple lovers as there are many unusual colors in these rugs from India that set them off well, like lavender, green, copper, and beige. I suggest that you look at a number of flat-surfaced wool dhurrie rugs if you are considering a modern lavender room. Take a look at the colors and the way they are combined. In fact, dhurries are hard to use in a room unless you start the color scheme from the rug.

Modern lavender-loving people like plants in white sculpted pots and may set a table with a centerpiece of white candles in white-painted pots. Often they like things somewhat Victorian, like their purple-loving elders. They sometimes choose Victorian furniture with frames painted white and seats covered in a lavender rose. They like white-painted dining tables of the klutzy Victorian type and like to set that table with white lace placemats and white porcelain.

In a modern purple room with Victorian accents, I see lavender as an edging color to use with white. I see painted floors with stenciled bouquets of lavender African violets entwined with green ribbon. Lavender and red is another good combination. I like a burgundy-colored wall with lavender sofas and an Oriental rug with dark burgundy, blue, and beige. Oriental rugs work well with lavender.

I recently did an apartment in the Art Deco style using white and lavender satin. My client had a white-painted piano, and I gave her chromium Art Deco stools with lavender satin tops. It was definitely Harlowesque. She also had a lavender chaise longue and Art Deco accessories including lavender frosted glass. She loved lace-on-lace over lavender satin, so at the windows we took old tablecloths and made window drapery out of them. Underneath she had a lavender satin draw drapery of one panel to close out the darkness. The lace-tablecloth curtain was on a rod and was tied back with a lavender bow.

Lavender requires proper lighting, because it can go very gray and dark at night. It requires a lot of sparkle. It's good with light fixtures that are tiny strings of draped lights similar to Christmas tree lights. Lavender doesn't do well under harsh light or a spotlight that floods an area.

Orange

Orange is the hardest color to use in home decorating. I've seen fewer rooms in orange, especially bright orange, than in any other color. Nevertheless, orange used correctly can be stunning.

Fire orange is one of those fabulous orange shades that really lights up a room when used properly. It is the strongest of the orange colors and comes from only one place on earth, Bangkok, Thailand. In the Far East the environment *is* paprika.

Opulent color is not an accent there, it predominates. As in the style of the French Louis, the opulent is not only in appropriate taste, it is a requirement. Rich, bright orange works in Thai silk with its high-gloss luster as do shocking pink and gleaming aquamarine. The Thais make a shocking pink, shocking orange, and white plaid that's fantastic.

The hue of opulent orange is not warm but fiery. It almost shines like a stone, as if it were jewelry. There aren't many truly orange stones. If you visit a museum's mineral collection you will see many shockingly brilliant gems, but you won't see a fire orange. This orange is a sun color. There is nothing at all of the earth in it. The closest we can come is in the lustrous finish of Jim Thompson Thai silk.

Orange is the brightest and most intense color there is. It has more fire than red. Most people water orange down to salmon, melon, or apricot, but rarely use it in its full intensity. I think the reason it's rarely used in home decorating is because orange-loving people are generally believed to be on the *gauche* side and often they go for a lively look but end up with dull walls. The truth is that orange as a paint in a flat texture does not have the necessary iridescence. You have to go to fabric or wallpaper for fire orange. Nothing else will quite do.

To do a room in fire orange, I would begin with a bright kumquat shantung fabric on the walls and paint all the woodwork a cream beige. The backs of the beige built-in bookcases I would lacquer with a black brown. The carpet could be an English-type tweed with a little fleck of orange in it and a border in black brown. I would then bring in a black-brown English Chesterfield sofa tufted in leather and add a beautiful Chinese Coromandel screen on one wall. Other accessories in this kumquat room might be delicate Chinese tables with painted figures on black lacquer and edged in gold. I would also find a pair of gleaming orange porcelain lamps. This is a Far

Eastern accent color that is readily available. There is a wide selection to choose from in lamps that have a black background with kumquat-orange figures. The cream-colored shades for the lamps should match the beige in the woodwork and built-ins.

On these beige-painted bookcases with the black-brown backs I would display a set of Chinese porcelains that have a fire orange in their pattern. Porcelains with bisque-colored backgrounds and Thai-orange designs are not difficult to find. I would use orange Thai fabric with a beige and black check or a plaid in tones of orange. Remember there must be an iridescence to the color of fire orange. It has to be silk to have the proper luster or it won't work in this Far Eastern room.

For a coffee table I would choose one in a linen texture painted the same color as the orange walls and then lacquered. I like wood surfaces covered with linen, which is glued down to give a kind of rush-matting surface that is also smooth. I would use some wonderful sculpted gold Siamese heads on black bases as accent pieces in this orange room. I would also use the lustrous silk plaid fabric for curtains and hang them on poles painted beige.

There's a great sophistication to orange when it's used correctly. I think the reason few people use it is they don't know how. Many people will use orange in their kitchens, however, perhaps because they associate it with the popular kitchen wallpaper featuring apples and oranges. Often this paper inspires them to paint the trim in their kitchen orange. They would be better off painting the trim to match the white or cream-colored background in the wallpaper.

Orange may be a difficult color, but it goes well with pine. It is one of the colors that can make wood really look burnished. One of the prettiest tones one can find in pine is a certain pinkish-orangey glow that's closer to amber than henna. Old pine has almost a fiery orange cast that goes well with orange.

Here is an orange country kitchen that takes advantage of the look of pine and the way it enhances orange. I would begin by painting the walls a bittersweet orange with cream trim, and I would have a chocolate-brown or coffee-colored ceiling with wide beams. There are a great many bittersweet-colored fabrics on the market. For the seats of window chairs around a big pine table with a lazy Susan on the top, I would find a small print of bittersweet orange and goldenrod. Then I would find a goldenrod-and-orange woven fabric for the seat of a wing chair pulled up to the fire. I see the room taking on even more character with the addition of green-and-white porcelain or blue-and-white stoneware. Brown-and-white stoneware would also look fabulous.

If there's room for it, this kitchen could accommodate a country settle. All the cabinets could be pine with interiors the same color as the walls. If you're lucky and are able to find a lot of old American country shelves and cabinets, they could be used instead of kitchen cabinets with closed fronts. I like to see old-fashioned cabinets used in country kitchens with the old wood shelves removed and replaced with glass. Then, if the interiors are lighted, the light can reflect down on all the pretty china and glassware.

Black

Rarely do people choose black as their favorite color, and those who do may either be succumbing to a temporary mood swing or a love of the extreme statement.

It used to be that black received a no rating of 100 percent on color-preference tests. That's no longer so. While men like it more than women do, the dislike rating has dropped to 90 percent, and that remaining 10 percent is a sophisticated lot. When used to its best advantage, the black room conveys an atmosphere of distinction, elegance, even nobility, especially if it's the shiny black of lacquer, ebony, or marble.

The black-to-gray room is back in vogue. People are fascinated by it. The black room is supposed to awaken your sensitivity to mystery. It has become possible to decorate in black because of technical advancements in lighting. You could take a cave today, light it, and make it glamorous. People who want a black room are generally of the avant garde, those who want the latest that technology has to offer.

Lovers of black like to live high up, the higher the better. They love having a great view of the city lit up all around them. I generally think of black rooms as media-oriented with a lot of chrome and advanced sound systems that also come in black. Black-loving people like black vertical blinds, for a window treatment, that open and shut at the press of a button. They may cover their walls in a black ribbed grass cloth and buy a black sectional sofa. The one touch of color may be a plant in a chrome pot, usually a fern (the most primitive kind of plant). Black-loving people sometimes have linen-covered, black-lacquered end tables. They buy big Lucite lamps, because they like the way the light shines on the plastic and the effect that it makes against the black wall. They also like opaque shades perforated with pinpoints in the style of antique pierced tin but more modern in feeling. They like a big piece of sculpture on a Lucite base, beautifully lighted, and a huge coffee table with a black marble top and rolled base.

In general, lovers of black tend to buy things overscale and fill rooms with upholstered architecture. Their dining-room table might display black china and candles in low chrome candlesticks. They might also have indirect lighting that washes the entire table.

Black-loving people like huge ashtrays made of a good, heavy smoked glass on the coffee table. They entertain a lot but rarely have time for domestic activity. Fortunately there are fast-food shops around where they can buy ready-made pasta and cheese or curried chicken salad on the way home from work and arrange it beautifully on a lacquered Chinese tray.

Black-loving people also like black bathrooms with black tubs and sleek black, reflective Carrara marble. They like the Art Deco style in cut-glass shower doors and big, round, glossy pottery vases for vivid sprays of gladioli. The reason they like gladioli, especially the red, is that they make one enormous statement.

There is a black-loving person with an appreciation of the Orient who is altogether different from the jet-set lover of black. There is a mystique about lovers of the black Oriental style. They might have black walls, a gold-painted ceiling, gold chairs with black satin upholstery, and serve fantastic dinners with pomegranates in a priceless bowl as a centerpiece. Or they might serve Peking duck on a clear glass plate.

I have done lots of black rooms in my time and recently did a powder room in black for a Polish count and countess. I used a shiny black embossed wallpaper in a modern treatment of a Chinese coin design. The carpet was black as were all the fixtures and the hardware was black onyx and dipped gold. I used a lot of mirrors on the walls and a lot of glass accents. The countess was of French birth and she bought some interesting flower prints for the walls that I thought were incongruous for the style she wanted. She said that in order to make the room feel right for herself in the daylight she needed to put the flower prints up. Although she used her apartment for entertaining at night, she used it for herself during the day. I mounted the flower prints in gold-edged black glass frames with mirror mattings.

The modern black bedroom is one that often appears on the covers of *Architectural Digest.* It can be duplicated in your own environment, with some changes. The walls of the magazine's typical dream bedroom in black might be covered in a slick textured wall covering like an alternating black glossy and textured stripe. The headboard might be of a shiny black fabric tufted in four-inch squares. The bed would never have a loose skirt but would be upholstered around the box spring so that it almost looked like a platform or the base of a sofa.

The sheets would be postmodern gray in a gray-on-gray pattern. The pillowcases could be gray with a little bit of black trim. The carpet could be industrial gray with a loop, the kind you find a lot in offices. The bedroom should look almost like a working space. In fact, there could be a desk with a top of black Carrara marble or black lacquer in the room. It might be on a Lucite frame to give it a floating look, although the desk might have a drawer or two. The light fixture would be black also, modern Italian in feeling, and the light would be set at an angle. Or the fixture might be a bulb in a frosted tone hanging from a cord.

A black-loving person might have an armless chaise in the room, because the black-loving person does not want to feel encroached upon. The bed floats for the same reason. The chaise could have low end tables on each side and the lighting could be indirect from hidden surface-mounted spots, with small tensor lights provided for reading. The ceiling could be black or mirrored. It would not be smoke-mirrored, because that would be too Venetian in feeling, but it might be done in strips of clear glass or, better yet, block glass.

As far as plants go in this room, I doubt there would be one, but if there were, it would be something severe and chic like a California cactus. This room would most likely have a big media screen, the biggest available, so that the only color in the room would come from the television set.

The connecting bathroom, if money were no object,

would feature black marbleized surfaces with gray veins. The bath towels would be black and gray with monograms in reverse colors—black on gray and gray on black. The jewelry appointments in this postmodern black bath would be silver. The stone would be black onyx. The window treatment could be black screen shades or black vertical blinds.

White

The white room is the most sought-after color scheme today. Of the clients I've had who wanted me to do all-white rooms I remember one in particular. She was from Philadelphia, and she wanted a dead-white carpet, which is very hard to find. Sample after sample was presented but none was white enough for her. Bleached wool when dyed is never the stark white color she desired. It will always have a slight flaxen hue. The woman from Philadelphia wanted a drop-dead white room in the Jean Harlow style, being a blonde herself. "The colors of white in these rug samples look like a dirty white dog," she said. The only way the kind of white-white look she had in mind can be achieved in a rug is to buy a white bearskin or other white fur and risk offending animal lovers.

The woman from Philadelphia who wanted an all-white bedroom was a little woman and very pristine in her taste and manner. I rarely find big people favoring white. They know it makes them look even bigger. But there are several kinds of white-loving people who like the Continental style. They are very different from the white-loving people who like the modern look. The Continental white room is filled with many small accessories and precious bibelots. There are lots of end tables with glass tops through which one can look down at collections on shelves below. Continental white lovers favor Chinese jades, snuff bottles, French furniture on the small scale, chairs with carved wood frames, cut-crystal lamps with pleated shades, and wall hangings in groups, generally framed in gold and white with silk matting.

White-loving people like a sophisticated plant like a big handsome jade. They're not fond of ferns or common philodendron. They like the rug-on-rug look and like to put down a big white rug with a small Persian prayer rug under the coffee table.

Some white-loving people like their walls ice-cream white and their draperies white damask with a gold trim. They may go for a celadon or a pale rose wall, but generally not blue. They like crystal chandeliers and night tables that are painted white and gold. They like white bedspreads on the bed and like to turn them down at night. If a bed doesn't have a bedspread, to them it's not finished. They like closets with white-and-gold-foil wallpaper and brass rods for their hangers. They love built-ins and mirrors to reflect even more white on white.

White-loving people like hand-painted murals or scenic wallpaper murals. But they don't like to live with colors that are subdued. They like white opaline jars with bronze tops and cigarette lighters on the table. White-loving people always have a spotless kitchen. They love vermeil, footed coffee cups, porcelains (but never birds), and figurines of the early Dresden variety. They like bronze wall sconces and love marble and marbleized-vinyl floors.

Joan Crawford was a famous white lover, but not in the French style. She was typical of some white-loving people who go in for a more modern look, in that she had a strong desire to look as if she had "arrived." I have noticed that people who need to show that they have made it have usually come a long way, and their experiences give them a great need for order, pristine cleanliness, and light. Joan Crawford, as everyone must know by now, was a super-neatnik. She wanted everything in her life just so. She lined up her shoes by color and stored her accessories in color-coded boxes. All her backgrounds were white with the exception of her bedroom, which was light pink. She had everything in perfect order in her closets. She wanted the hat shelf lined up with the bag shelf lined up with the shoe shelf lined up with the glove shelf, and those shelves were also color coded. If she planned to wear pink on a certain day the ensemble would be selected from color-coordinated storage units. Joan Crawford, like many super-orderly white-loving people, had to have everything as close to perfect as possible.

The truly modern white-loving person is totally different from the Joan Crawford type. Modern white rooms have come about because of the invention of plastic laminate. When this white washable surface, common in schools and offices, was introduced into the home it made possible the built-in or semi-built-in room, the kind where everything is available in modules—and is cheap. The white room is thought by many to exemplify the contemporary look. Some people believe that if you paint your rooms white, lay down a white rug, bring in a white sofa, and use accents of purple and black the environment will sing "now." What it will sing is "plastic." Using white is not as easy as all that.

White *is* easy to use in a room that is pared-down, bare, and easy to care for. Such a room gives people, clothing, and accessories a chance to stand out. Some of my favorite kinds of white rooms are inspired by Marimekko, a designer who had a wonderful sense of color in fabrics. I love some of her Scandinavian designs—big black waves against green, or bright purple with a pink flower. These vivid fabrics look very good used against white. The fabric can be bought by the yard or framed and hung on the wall. The white room conveys a youthful look. It's a contemporary look that works for what I call transient living, whether used to furnish a first apartment or a beach house. Because the white machine-made furniture has little craftsmanship to it, it is not expensive and gives rooms a feeling of unity.

The white living room in the Continental style is also very orderly. Here the white carpet can have a bit of a tawny shade to it. The walls might be covered in a white silk string fabric with a slight texture. The curtains could be sheer white, silky and filmy. This is especially effective for wonderful views high up. There might be a curved-back sofa covered in a white silk with a slub, such as shantung. The sofa could be tufted with a skirt. Next to the sofa might be a pair of marble-topped tables with light fruitwood bases in the French manner. On the tables I would use lamps made from white cut-crystal glass vases on gold bases with white silk shades. There could be a glass-topped coffee table with a bronze doré base. On the table might be an egg-shaped cigarette lighter of cut crystal with a matching ashtray. A pair of pull-up benches with crisscross bases covered in a white silk could accompany the grouping. Or you could use a pair of French fauteuils with walnut frames covered in a white-on-white stripe. Next to one of the chairs might be a Japanese garden bench.

In the same white room might be a card table with four chairs with white and gold frames, the seats covered in celadon green. There could be a server on that table on which sits a silver or vermeil coffee service or a small doré tray filled with little sherry glasses and hock glasses of green, blue, purple, and red. Over the card table there could be a crystal chandelier.

Here is a white bedroom for the modern lover of white. The walls might be dead-white, perhaps in a textured material like stucco, or covered in a white grass cloth. The ceiling might be white lacquer. On the floor might be a white Berber wool rug or a diamond-sculpted carpet with a smooth surface so that it could be kept very clean. The lover of white almost never chooses shag. To go with a fully upholstered architectural headboard there could be a linen bedskirt fully lined in white cotton batiste. On the bed might be a white linen-and-cotton quilt with an embroidered border and many pillows in white cases with tailored edges.

There might be two straight chairs in the room made of a highly polished metal with white tweed covers. There could also be one comfortable armchair with an ottoman also in the white tweed. On the walls could be brilliant Matisse or Gauguin prints, Impressionistic pastels, or the latest drop-dead painting from a SoHo gallery. White becomes the background in such a room for the display of something wonderful.

Brown

Brown is another complicated color when it comes to meaning, because it contains a combination of all the primary colors: yellow, red, and blue. In combination, the bright qualities of the pure colors are toned down to a great extent. Gone is the expansive quality of yellow and the excitation of red. What remains is a passive yet receptive color that, like the soil, has "roots." Brown is a physical color that promotes feelings of security, contentment, and safety. It's the color of trees, which have always provided human shelter.

Brown is a color men like more than women, who almost never pick brown rooms. I've never done a room in brown for a woman, although I came close to doing one recently. It would have had brown glazed walls, white trim, and furniture in beige silky tones. All this was to be the background for a collection of blue-and-white porcelain. This client had chosen a contemporary carpet of beige with a dash of brown. Accompanying Louis XIV carved console tables were large ornate mirrors and solid-blue porcelains. But my client changed her mind. She decided not to use the brown walls and chose instead a fawn color deeper than a tan. I believe the room would have been more striking with the darker tone of brown with the blue-and-white porcelains, but she said she couldn't live with brown walls. The tawny color she chose was still very attractive and went well with a large chandelier in bronze doré with crystal trim.

I really don't know why women don't like brown rooms. They often don't want to live in the brown wood-paneled room either. Whenever I do a traditional library for a female client, she invariably wants the woodwork bleached. A dark brown library may be fine for a man, but women don't like the heaviness of it. However, women do like brown tortoiseshell used in bamboo blinds. In other words, they like touches of brown but not too much.

Brown and pastels are a great combination in the bedroom: rich deep brown walls, white trim, and a floral chintz with big cabbage roses in reds, pinks, yellows, and peaches with green leaves on a yellow background. I would use a yellow carpet and a yellow quilted bed against the wall with children's portraits hung above it and skirted tables of yellow and pink on either side. Brown works well with lavender, peach, light blue, and pale green. Brown and green is a very good combination for most people, because, I believe, it is so treelike.

After a good rain, look at the color of the earth. That's the color brown to use in your home, not dry-soil brown. That color to me is a nothing-color, except in its natural setting, the Southwest, where it does work. In the Southwest you can bring a Navaho clay brown indoors with a touch of sky blue, rust, beige, and green. Clay brown works best with a creamy contrast. Dark brown looks best with a sharp contrast such as white or bright yellow. I would not use dried-earth brown with anything but creams, particularly in the Southwest.

Brown is a strong color, and when you weaken its strength too much it can create many problems in home decorating. If you plan to use brown, be daring. Think about browns that are the color of chocolate bars, tree bark, rich coffee or furs, and deeply tanned leather. With these strong, earthy browns, use paprika, grass green, lemon yellow, sky blue, and lots of white. These colors will make the room less earthbound. Bright red is another color that adds excitement and luster to brown. Remember that when you use brown in a room, you're only beginning. This is even more true with the use of beige, the popular paled-down version of brown that is the most ubiquitous shade in home decorating. Brown needs warming colors. It needs lots of cheerful color company. Pale pink, lettuce green, melon, and rich purple all do wonderful things to brown.

Here is a living room with brown as the predominant color, spruced up with some companion colors that warm and enliven it. This room, which is on the rustic side, would have earth-brown vinyl flooring, white stucco walls, and a beamed ceiling. Two couches could be covered in a floral print of orange, yellow, and white with touches of scarlet and gold. Yellow or gold pillows could provide accents. To warm the room further, I would choose a coffee table and end tables in a lacquer finish of cinnabar or mandarin orange.

Many people find themselves faced with the need to decorate a brown room, because the walls of that room are paneled in wood. If you have such a room, particularly if it is dark wood, you need to give that brown a lift. Choose fabrics and accessories in persimmon, sky blue, gold, zinnia red, plum, leafy green, and lots of white. These colors will make that room bright and cheerful. Use lamps of a canary-yellow porcelain and lots of plants in white or natural clay pots.

The Neutrals

The neutral colors are generally considered to be beige, gray, white, and ecru, but I much prefer the softer colors that can also be used as neutrals. A soft yellow, for instance, is a color that goes with everything: rust, camel, light blue, cottage pink, delphinium blue, navy blue, black, peach, bright red, rich mid-summer green. There's almost nothing that you can put against that soft yellow that won't work.

The same is true for soft pink. Take, for instance, a pink shirt worn by a man with a navy-and-red-striped tie. There's nothing unmasculine about light pink, and there's a glow to pink that's good for men's skin, too. I can take the colors of a man's suit, shirt, and tie ensemble and use those colors in a masculine-oriented one-room studio apartment. I would paint the walls white with a touch of pink in them, the color of men's shirts, and I would paint the ceiling white. Then I would put down a navy-red-and-white-striped carpet on the floor. This carpet could be laid on the diagonal. Then I might buy a sectional sofa covered in navy and accented with red, white, and mattress-ticking-pink pillows. At the windows I would use the same ticking stripe hung on navy-blue poles. The effect of this room is at the same time very masculine and very neutral.

The most "neutral" of all to me is a very soft sky blue with just a hint of green, a very light blue. I have found that blue is the color that most people find the least offensive, which makes it an ideal neutral. When a couple discusses room color, blue is one that seems to end up at the top of the list of their mutual choices. It seems to be the color most people can live with, perhaps because it's the universal color. We walk under it every day. With this clear sky blue I like some earth color like dark green. This earth-and-sky color combination is in my experience one of the most popular color choices. Sky blue can be used as a background color for nearly every other color.

Thomas Jefferson painted the undersides of the porticoes of Monticello this soft aqua-tinted light blue. A blue that has too much gray or white can be very severe, but a blue that has just a little touch of aqua makes me think of the sunlit waters of Sardinia or the Greek isles of the Aegean.

The pastels of Palm Beach are a range of neutral shades that are particular favorites of a lot of people. These include sun-washed yellow, light pink, soft beige, soft blue, and light lavender and are always used with white trim. There's even a white-on-white that could be called pastel in a sunny clime like Palm Beach.

When I think about the big Renaissance-style stucco houses of Palm Beach, I think of soft gray with white and soft azalea with white. There's something very cooling about these neutral pastels in hot climates. Were a house painted in deep blue, deep pink, or bright yellow, the brilliance would come across as hard looking.

If you were to do a New York or Chicago environment where you had lots of windows and light, you might try a pastel look that would work the way it does in the tropics. The pastel look is also quite French, but it doesn't work in English interiors, and pastels don't make it at all in an Oriental-style room.

However, you might use French pastels in an urban apartment on a high floor with lots of light that will give an airy look to the colors. You could paint the walls a soft shell pink and put shell-pink damask drapery bordered in a simple beige at the windows. The lining of the drapes could be a rose-colored print. The carpet in this shell-pink room with shell-pink draperies could also be soft shell pink, but in a Chinese style with a border of light blue and soft green. The upholstery in the room could be white with a silk stripe. The pillows could be round or square. The round ones could be in the soft damask pink and the square ones in a soft teal green with a white border. The furniture in the room could be French in style, painted a pale, pale green. The top of the case goods could be white marble.

There should be a lot of light in such a room, and by that I mean reflected light. For example, one wall in this living room could be completely mirrored, and on the mirrored wall could be hung another mirror in a graceful French style with a painted green frame with a touch of silver. The sconces above the white marble fireplace could also be silver and have soft pink shades. The glow of this pastel pink would give this room a kind of in-the-clouds feeling. The ceiling would be tinted soft pink, so that when the light reflected down it would cast a pretty pink glow on the white silk sofas. At the windows under the damask draperies could be white silk Austrian shades that are very light and bouffant in feeling.

When you are decorating in a contemporary vein and want to think in terms of pastels but don't like French furniture, here's a combination of colors that may work for you. Begin by painting all the walls a very soft pastel blue. The moldings could be a soft banana cream. With these blue walls and the banana-cream ceiling, you could use a banana cream and soft blue geometric carpet, preferably one of the English carpets that has a loop to it. Or you could choose a pale blue loop carpet with a dash of banana cream. You might upholster your sofas in a soft blue durable fabric like a raw Bangkok silk that you could accent with banana cream and soft blue pillows. When it comes to furniture for your creamy blue room, you could use end tables covered in linen. You might choose see-through lamps such as those made of large pieces of Plexiglas shaped like diamonds or rectangles, so that you could see the blue through the lamp. Use soft colors and glass for accents. Ashtrays could be ceramic in the banana-cream shade and sit on banana-cream tables. For upholstery I would use chairs with fretwork backs so that, as with the lamps, you could look through them to the blue walls. The seats of the chairs could be done in solid blue and banana cream. I like the serenity of rooms that have a unified color scheme.

There are rooms that you can decorate in one color and one color alone. You can take any color: beige, peach, blue, gray, and with accent pieces—paintings, lamps, and accessories —make it work. There are many people who like the one-color decorating idea. It makes them feel put together. I've seen apartments and houses that were done one color, such as blue or peach with a touch of beige or white.

As exciting and complex as the nine major colors are— blue, red, yellow, green, orange, purple, brown, black, and white—whether you use them full strength or in their whited-down neutral state, they are even more exciting and complex in combination, which is where color magic begins.

Color Magic

Many people think that decorating begins with furniture, the layout of a house or apartment, or the selection of carpets and light fixtures. All these things are important, of course, but I believe the basic element in decorating is color. It is the most magical of all decorating tools. By magical I mean that it reveals and evokes much more than meets the eye. What you think about color, how it affects you, and how you use it can make an environment come to life and be very expressive.

Before you select colors, you need to know the meanings of colors. These meanings are often universal; that is, they are remarkably the same in all cultures. Response to colors is similar no matter where a person lives or whether that person is young or old, male or female. The properties of colors have less to do with their pigments than with the accumulation of meanings that have been associated with them since time immemorial. No matter how modern your approach in decorating, it's important to know that there is a tradition of meaning behind every color that you choose, even in the most up-to-date modern environments.

These color meanings have been the subject of many scientific tests. I find the results fascinating, because they confirm the results of my own very unscientific observations over the years to determine color preferences in my clients.

The Psychology and the Physiology of Color

When I work with children, I see an approach to color that is totally natural. For instance, one day my young son Sebastian came home from kindergarten and showed me a painting he had done in school. I noticed that he was beginning to show a strong interest in expressing himself through colors and asked him, "What colors would you like in your room?"

"I'll make you a picture of what I want," he said. In his picture he had red, blue, yellow, green, brown, black, orange, and purple, all in the bright paint-box colors. At first his walls were painted blue like the sky, and then he continued to color until the painting of his room ended up the color of mud. Not pleased with the final outcome, he started a new picture.

If adults want to understand their emotional responses to color, they need only observe how children approach color. Studies done on preschool children show that it's the children who have a strong emotional orientation who emphasize color. Red, which is the universally preferred color among adults (half the flags of the independent nations of the world are predominantly red), is also the color preferred by children during their early preschool years. Then children grow out of their hotly impulsive stage and into one where they gradually learn to control those emotions while increasing their intellectual response. They begin to develop an interest in the cooler colors. Their second color choice is rational blue.

Children who emphasize blue at a very early age are found to be concerned with control of both themselves and others. However, in the natural course of development, children will frequently turn to blue as they begin to concentrate on form and the control of line and outgrow their previous preoccupation with swooping masses of color. The finger-painting stage is the time to develop those deep emotional responses to color. If you have never finger-painted, or haven't done so in years, I recommend it. If you really want to get into the emotionally charged subject of color, your sensory response can be enhanced by the feel of color between the fingers and the way it smears onto the paper. Such indulgences can be made discreetly if there is a preschool-age child in your world to finger-paint with.

By the time children reach first grade they have become more sophisticated in their color choices. They are past the primary-color phase and into the secondaries. The size of their box of color crayons must now go beyond the original eight or they won't be able to discover the full palette. Studies done on children of this age have found that girls are better at differentiating colors than boys (which I have observed is also true in adults when it comes to the more subtle hues) and all children have some trouble distinguishing between the light and the dark shades of a particular color.

Another group of studies concerning children and creativity suggests that the color-oriented child is more likely to become an artistic adult, someone who likes to do creative and innovative work. Conversely, these studies suggest that the child who is more concerned with form than color will grow up to pursue more factual matters, more quantitative than emotional.

The body's response to color can be measured by increased heart rate, blood pressure, and breathing. Red is an exciting color—literally—as it excites the nervous system. Blood pressure goes up. Respiration and heart rate increase. Blue has the opposite effect on the nervous system. Exposure to blue causes blood pressure to fall, heart rate and breathing to slow down. Interestingly, blue is the color of the absence of blood. All these physiological responses to color take place below the threshold of awareness, which is what makes our response to color much more than what merely meets the eye. These bodily responses to color can't be ignored. Whether we are aware of them or not, colors affect how we feel.

It has been found that hospitals with a monotonous color scheme cause a deterioration in the ability of patients and staff to concentrate. People are more prone to suffer lapses of attention. Libraries are sometimes done in a combination of calming and jolting colors. One color produces an overall atmosphere of quietude, while the color accents wake up those who would otherwise nod over their books. Another test has revealed that depressed people have a strong preference for bright, gay colors, perhaps to compensate for their bleak state of mind. Recently researchers found that shocking bubble-gum pink had a calming effect on institutionalized psychiatric patients, a color most healthy people would find nauseating.

Still another interesting color survey shows that as people climb up the social ladder, they select pastels over primary or secondary colors. Perhaps these upwardly mobile people don't need as much stimulation from their environment as they did when they lived a more homebound life. Now they require tranquillity at home.

Tests made on college students show that they generally see red, yellow, and orange as associated with excitement, stimulation, and aggression. Blue and green, on the other hand, are associated in their minds with calmness, serenity, and peace. Black and brown and gray are seen as colors of melancholy and depression. Yellow is associated with cheerfulness and a sunny disposition. Purple is adjudged dignified and royal, if a bit sad. Young people of college age often get their first decorating experience with the walls and ceiling of their college dormitory room. The decor may be shocking, but it's supposed to be. It is my clear memory that people of college age do very little sleeping. They need a stimulating environment in which to keep awake long enough to study.

Adolescents in their rebellious phases will often choose unacceptable colors (unacceptable, that is, to their parents) like a Day-Glo orange or purple ceiling with one red wall and one yellow wall. I have seen adolescents' rooms that broke all the rules of color choice. However, adolescent decorating schemes are of a transitory nature and can sometimes be amusing. I once saw a stucco ceiling in a dormitory room where each point of the stucco was tipped in one of three Day-Glo colors.

I had to admire the amount of work that had gone into it.

From childhood to full adulthood, color responses are more tied to the emotions than to rational thought-processes. People do not respond to colors with their intellect, but with deeper, earlier, learned responses, emotional and sensory. This is why color responses can be so erratic and unpredictable. Who knows why one person loves yellow and another hates it? Because of the unpredictable nature of color response, much research has been done by packagers on what people think of when they see specific colors. After all, the motto of the packaging industry is, "A package that draws attention to itself is half sold." However, drawing attention is not enough. A package must also inspire confidence in the consumer to part with his or her money. Researchers will tell you, based on their studies, that white conveys an image of purity and trust. It is understood to mean refreshing and antiseptic, especially in the proximity of blue. Think of the Ivory soap wrapping, which hardly has changed since the product was introduced. Red, of course, is an important advertising color because it stimulates the strongest body response in the beholder. The darker the red, researchers say, the more serious the product. The lighter the red, the more happy are the associations.

Pink is a sweet and romantic color. It is right for an intimate product, especially a cosmetic. It is also the preferred color in stomach medicine. As with the psychiatric patients' response to bubble-gum pink, no one knows quite why stomach-medicine pink elicits a calming effect on the upset consumer, but it seems to do so.

Color researchers have found that orange is the color that inspires communication. It radiates and is warm and inviting. Blue is an enhancer of other colors and widely used as such. On the Ivory soap package, the proximity of blue makes white look even more pure. Eggs with white shells sell best in a package with blue stripes. The egg content of mayonnaise is also enhanced by blue on the label, as blue makes the product look more yellow. White sheets look whiter in a blue package. So does sugar. Blue grains in a box of laundry detergent inspire the consumer to believe that there is extra-strength cleaning power in those blue granules.

Some colors are unsuitable for certain packaging because of the sensory responses they evoke in the realms of taste, smell, temperature, or weight (yes, colors even have an emotional weight to them). For instance, you might buy a pink beauty product, but you would not buy a biscuit in a pink package. Pink in food packaging is limited to frosting and other sweet things. A packager will tell you that it's a children's color, because for children nothing can be too sweet. A room can become too sweet, however, from an overdose of pink or the use of a too-bright pink. Used with cooling colors, however, pink can give a warming glow to a room.

Certain colors are to be avoided in packaging. You won't find a gray package, except in the most trendy postmodern packaging. You will never find a gray beauty cream. The reason, say the packagers, is that gray is a "nothing" color. It conveys lack of energy. At a deeper level, it conveys fear of old age. Other colors are inappropriate in different ways. You'll never find Louisiana hot sauce in a sky-blue package, just as you won't find caffeine-free coffee packaged in red. Decaffeinated coffee is carefully packaged so as not to appear too stimulating.

There are other color restrictions based on the sensory responses of taste and smell. For instance, you won't find candy bars sold in yellow-green or green-yellow packages because those colors convey acid reactions in the mouth via the eyes. Candy-bar wrappers are more likely to be in the orange-to-yellow-to-red range. Supersweet pink would never be used to package lemon products. Bitter-tasting colors are navy blue, brown, olive, and violet. Purple gentian conveys a special bitterness. Indigo is sour and bitter. These astringent colors mix well with sweet colors and less well with acid colors, just as in cooking. Salty colors are in the heather category, the green and blue of the ocean and the seashore, the gray of the dunes. Salt-and-pepper tweed is an example of salty coloring. Put salt with a little sweet and you will have a tasty color combination. Remember that the taste of color is a sensory matter. Reason has something but not everything to do with it.

There is a group of colors that have been found to stimulate the appetite. Those colors are citrus orange, lime green, clear yellow, bright vermilion, silver brown, and chocolate brown. Much will be made of these colors later in this book when we discuss decorating the dining room and, to a lesser extent, the kitchen. Color on the table also stimulates the appetite, and against any of the above appetite-stimulating colors, the all-time favorite color choice for china—blue and white—looks attractive.

Colors also have a smell. Piquant orange has a peppery or spicy odor. Green has the same spicy odor only less pronounced and more on the pine side. The perfumed colors are violet and lilac. Like too much perfume, too much violet and lilac can be a little sickening in a room. The antidote is more light and greenery. The combination of violet-to-lilac-to-lavender with white and green is stunning.

Many institutional dining rooms are painted orange. One wall might be bright orangey-orange and the next wall vermilion. Maybe those colors help work up an appetite for collegiate-school stew and maybe they don't, but at least the sensory receptors have something to keep them occupied. Remember that these colors are tapping deep emotions and do not reflect highly refined adult tastes.

You could stimulate the appetite in a more subtle way with pale celadon green walls. Or you could use a wallpaper with a celadon background in which ivy in spring green is mixed in an overall pattern with a vertical stripe of gold. Maybe you have a collection of delicate silver-brown translucent china or Benningtonware. Silver brown and chocolate brown both stimulate the appetite and look good against celadon. Or you might prefer the walls painted in a rich chocolate-cake brown, which looks so wonderful lit by candles. The trim might be banana cream. On the table might be unbleached linen and basketware, and the china might be that favorite blue and white. It's remarkably easy to decorate a dining room in colors that stimulate the senses.

Colors also register a physical weight in the mind. White and yellow register the lightest, and violet to black the heaviest. If you want to make a room seem lighter, the answer is simple, even if you're working with heavy pieces of furniture. Light-colored slipcovers in the summer are an age-old custom, and, I think, a good one. In the wintertime those deep shades of heavy violet and black might be a background against which you can warm yourself. However, when the seasons change and it's time to open the windows to the summer sky and green leaves, people experience a great desire to lighten up the home environment. The easiest way I know to lighten up is to pop on light-colored slipcovers over those warm, dark shades. Another way to lighten a room is to take up dark-colored, heavily patterned rugs in the summer. A light floor of pine or maple or bleached oak gives an airy feeling to a room and makes it feel brighter and cooler—and on a hot day that can make living more comfortable.

One color-preference test that I find particularly interesting was conducted on men and women living in North America. The subjects' order of preference was the following: blue, red, green, violet, orange, and yellow. Women show a slight preference for red over blue, and men for blue over red. This finding might reflect cultural identification, as the adult American men and women of today were most likely pink and blue babies. From the bassinet and the first layette, it's little-boy blue and little-girl pink. That wavering of preference for red and blue is to me like yin and yang, a counterbalance of colors, one too hot and the other too cool to use alone.

This study is interesting to me for another reason, and that is that orange is preferred over yellow by men and yellow over orange by women. This also corresponds to the preferences I have observed during my many years as a decorating consultant. There is one color both men and women can agree on however: they both dislike green yellow. Why is it then that America's favorite decorating color choice is avocado? Many studies have been undertaken by market researchers whose business it is to sell products through the mass media, and they all reveal the same order of preferences with the same gender differences, and *all* rate green yellow high on the dislike list. Sometimes I wonder if avocado wasn't a color in some decorator's bad dream who, when he woke up, created a color that became a permanent addition to the American decorating scene. What could be more permanent than the color of a refrigerator, bathtub, or wall-to-wall carpeting? How long does it take for an expensive avocado rug to wear out, people wonder. Yes, avocado is still around—that green-yellow color the experts say is the one most people agree to hate. The good news is that avocado is easy to brighten up and live with pleasurably.

Color Preferences

When I begin testing clients for color preference, I use several kinds of color tests. One is a stack of pictures that I go through one at a time while the client picks the ones that appeal. I often believe people are intimidated by the fact that someone is trying to find something out about them—to psych them out —so they begin to question themselves and wonder if they are indeed telling the truth. In order to avoid that confusion, I go through the stack of pictures and ask them to judge quickly whether they would want that picture in their home. The pictures that appeal go in one pile, and those that do not go in another. Generally there is a stream of color-consciousness in the preferred pile, one or more colors that appear again and again. That pile may include pinks with yellows with blues, and the discard pile may include oranges, beiges, and browns. Whatever the choice, my informal color-preference test gives my clients some definite clues about their preferences.

I know how carefully people pick china and how aware they are of what is pleasing to them. They know they are buying something they want to last a long time and that they will use more or less frequently. They are likely to take their color preferences seriously when choosing china, and I use their choices as clues to their color preferences.

I don't think people know their true color preferences until they mature later in life, around the age of fifty. Then people finally begin to know what colors are flattering to them and what is just an interesting but passing fancy.

Color Illusion

Color has many additional magical properties. Take color illusion. Did you know that color can drastically reduce bulk? One of the most amazing properties of color is its ability to do this. In the three-dimensional world of home decorating, the two most bulky items are the sofa and the bed. They are everybody's biggest decorating headache. If you wish to make your sofa and bed disappear, wave the magic wand of color and watch a melon-colored sofa blend into a melon-colored wall; watch a queen-size, azalea-colored bed become part of an azalea-colored wall. That is color magic. White sheets under that azalea bedspread might be trimmed in azalea and kumquat orange. You could accent the bed with cushions of kumquat orange on one side and azalea on the other.

When the color of the couch or the bed is the same color as the wall, the pieces are transformed from individual hunks of furniture to what is known as architectural furnishings— those that join together to become part of the background, whether they are built in or merged together by color.

If you want to try the architectural approach in your bedroom and/or living room, it's easy. I have found there are so many shades available in fabric and paint now that it is rarely a problem matching the two, and custom-mixed paint is the great adjuster. Once you have found your fabric, take it to the paint store and show it to the mixer. What appears on the color chart is just the beginning. What I suggest is that you take a gallon of paint home and streak each wall with a generous brushstroke or two, and then observe the color as the light changes, darkness comes, and night lights go on. Choosing the color of your walls is not so simple a matter as liking a particular gradation of hue on a paint-store color chart. It means watching that color in action as it interacts with the sun in your rooms and then reflects the artificial light of night. Alas, as you adjust the paint color, that perfect fabric may no longer be the perfect match with the walls. However, finding a better match is rarely a problem in this color-saturated age. On either end of the match, there is the possibility of adjustment. Once you have done this, you will find that your major living-room problem, the sofa, and your major bedroom problem, the bed, have more or less disappeared. Presto!

The bedroom mix-and-match process is similar to the living-room routine. Bedroom light is either early morning or late night, depending on how you use your bedroom. Fabrics for bedcovers come in swatches, so you can test the color out and see if you like what it does to your environment. Match that swatch to the painted wall and your big, bulky bed becomes part of the background, a focal point for pillows. This mix-and-match use of color is not only magic in the way that it solves bulk problems, it also creates an environment in which accessories gleam and glow. Accessory art makes a bigger statement in this harmonious setting, and many people like the feeling of unity, an all-together look, that their rooms have when they are treated this way.

Another magical aspect of color illusion used in decorating is the phenomenon called *figure on ground.* You, no doubt, have seen the classic example of black silhouettes against a white background where you either perceive two facing profiles (the figure) or the background (a vase). In the phenomenon of figure on ground, one or the other will stand out. Depending on many variables, including one's mental state at the time, either the figure or the ground will predominate. This is where the magic comes in.

People have a great need to create an environment around them that has a sense of unity and stability, a continuity of design that creates a feeling of closure without being closed in. Through the choice of colors you can determine whether you want that environment to be stimulating or calming, intimate or formal, cozy or expansive.

One of the ways to unify all the elements in a pleasing way is by the combination of color and pattern, or figure and ground. An environment carefully planned around color and pattern, figure and ground, can't help but be pleasing. In home furnishings, the ground is usually considered to be the carpet and walls, and can include the sofa and bed if they are the same color as the walls. The figure is the contrasting fabrics, wallpaper, and furniture. What happens when you put a patterned furniture-covering or a brightly colored lacquered end table against a medium-to-neutral-colored floor and wall? The figure will predominate over the wall. But, a wine-colored chair can be consumed by a dark floor and paneled walls and recede into the ground. Dark floors, however, can be used as an effective ground for the display of colorful patterned accessories such as Victorian hooked rugs or gleaming porcelain temple jars. If you want to use your floor as a ground and then emphasize it, color your walls in a similar shade. If you violate this rule, the eye becomes confused. For instance, if you have light-colored furniture and a light-colored floor covering, the walls alone have to balance out the figure-ground duet. The walls alone can't do this, so the eye wanders confusedly. However, if you limit the light-colored floor covering to a rug in pale Danish pastels under a grouping of your light-colored furniture, and around that rug you have a stained oak, rich teak, or dark pine floor, then you have established the parameters of figure and ground in a pleasing way. Although this style of decorating seems a simple thing when explained to someone in a room where it's been done successfully, it is not as easy as it looks. It requires that the home decorator make a choice about whether an element should be in the foreground or background. Make the wrong choice and you'll end up with too much going on. I find the best way to deal with the challenge is to make a strong color statement with the walls, define them neatly in white, and add another strong statement with the carpet. Against this well-defined ground can be placed as many as ten well-chosen colors and a few patterns: a geometric, a floral, and a stripe. Most people, I have found, need what psychologists call the "moorings" of a high figure-ground organization in their environment. They want their backgrounds to interact with their foregrounds harmoniously.

If you look at the most popular wall coverings, the same attachment that most people have to the well-defined, figure-ground design is reflected there. Most wallpapers have well-defined objects in pleasing geometric patterns, often joined by a vertical stripe. Many people like the definition to include the line between the wall and the ceiling. This can be done with a wallpaper border or contrasting molding. There are a few patterns of wallpaper in free-floating abstract designs, but much more popular are those that define space more precisely and clearly. However, there are pitfalls in designing a room that is too well defined. The too well defined room is too full of contrast, too hard. What can help break up and soften the look is a few carefully chosen objects.

Generally speaking, to achieve the artful balance of figure and ground, the warm colors (red- and yellow-based) tend to be figure, while the colors that we think of as cool (green-, blue-, or purple-based) are the ground. Black and white also serve as ground. The reason for this is that warm colors seem to "advance" while cool colors "recede." If you want to determine whether a color you are interested in joins the figure or the ground of your overall plan, put a swatch of it on the wall, or line up the colors you have chosen in fabric, paint, and wallpaper, look at them as a group, and see which recede and which advance. Doing this is easy enough, and you will find that the more you do it the more aware of color you will become. There are some colors that virtually leap out at one. Remember that one color that advances or recedes too much is not going to join in the well-defined space you are creating.

Colors in Combination

Some colors in combination enhance each other's separate qualities, while other colors may negate each other when placed side by side. For example, the combination of blue and gray provides an even more tranquil and peaceful mood than blue used alone. Blue and purple are still on the calm and peaceful side, but more stimulating and even erotic than blue used alone. Black when used with blue reinforces its peaceful aspect. Blue by itself tends to drift off into infinity, while green is more earthbound; used together they balance each other and give a feeling of orderly self-containment. Red and blue used together are harmonious but too active to promote the calm and peaceful effect of blue used alone.

Red and violet used together reinforce their individual qualities of sensory excitement. Black used with red changes the statement red makes from desire to drama, making red even more strong and forceful than when used alone. Yellow and red are the ultimate statement in brightness, for they are the two brightest colors. Yellow and violet is another of those fantastical combinations that stimulate the imagination and the desire for adventure. Yellow and black is a combination that is too strong for most tastes.

The combination of orange and black is directly connected in people's minds with Halloween. There are other color schemes that are too closely connected in most people's minds with holidays to provide a pleasant all-season atmosphere. Red and green will forever mean Christmas; frosting pink with yellow and icy blue mean Easter; brown with avocado and gold mean Thanksgiving; red, white, and pink mean Valentine's Day; green and white mean St. Patrick's Day; and red, white, and blue mean the Fourth of July. Many people enjoy holiday colors but worry about making their houses look like a holiday out of season. They are attracted to these color combinations and repelled by them at the same time. Easter colors to me are not a happy combination. Easter-egg colors can be quite sickening. There's something about the edible food-coloring colors that doesn't work for me except in frostings. I have seen rooms done in Easter colors with robin's-egg-blue walls and a frosting-pink carpet. The furniture frames were painted minty

Easter green. On the seats were a yellow-green-and-blue print. Accents were in lavender. There was something slightly nauseating about the room. No one wants to eat cake all day.

In order to change those too sweet and too Eastery colors from upsetting to pleasing, you could use the same color combinations but in different shades. For example, I would paint the room a very much softened light blue and the frames of the furniture white. I would choose a print with a light blue background with flowers of soft green, lavender, and rose pink. I would cover a pair of chairs in a deeper green chintz, and accent the sofa with the same green. I would put down a soft blue carpet. On the white coffee tables I would use white ceramic lamps with white silk shades. To use holiday colors well requires a light touch.

I love Christmas, but I'm always glad to take down the Christmas decorations, because the combination of all those colors becomes cloying after awhile. When you plan the color of your house, be sure to pick colors that will appeal to you for a long time. Remember how you feel about your Christmas decorations come the second week in January. There's only so much glitz and silver tinsel and popcorn balls tied with red ribbons that anyone can take. Colored lights are another example of too much of a good thing, because all the basic colors are there—red, blue, yellow, and green, in their brightest hues. Yet they work because Christmas is a once-a-year celebration and a little excess is what holidays are all about.

Full-Force Color

I find that there is no greater inspiration for choosing color than the natural world around us. Take, for example, the colors of a garden on a sunny day. There I might see zinnia reds, creamy roses, a daisy yellow, a delphinium purple, asparagus-fern green, camellia white, and a little touch of brilliant pollen orange in the centers of many of the flowers. Now, what is wrong with using all these colors in the same room? Many people would say that you can't do it, or shouldn't do it, because one color should predominate in a room. But I believe in taking garden colors and putting them *all* in an inside setting, with whatever period furnishings. The way successfully to incorporate these many shades of sunny garden colors in a room is to orchestrate them as carefully as a symphony—with the emphasis on *carefully*.

When planning such a room, I have to bear in mind what makes for an attractive flower garden. Suppose you have a garden of pink peonies, pink phlox, white phlox, blue delphinium, bluebells, and pink and white snapdragons, with a border of light blue sweet William. If you were to add to that garden bright orange marigolds and nasturtiums, the garden would clash. But the garden with marigolds would not clash if you also added some yellow and white daisies, yellow snapdragons, and yellow and red zinnias. The same principle is true for a room.

I have done a lot of rooms in my life that are called *full-force-color rooms*. In them, I use the rainbow of colors to express my opinion. Here is an example of a full-force-color room: The room would be painted my favorite sky blue with a white ceiling. The carpet might be a bright carnation red. It couldn't have too much blue in it, but must be bright and clear. I would paint all the trim and molding white. For drapery I would find an English country garden fabric with a white background. On it would be the panoply of floral colors: bouquets of pink roses, tulip colors in pinks and reds, blue delphiniums, yellow and white daisies, hollyhocks in pink and white, orange nasturtiums, and many shades of green.

These bouquets might be tied with a delphinium-blue ribbon.

Setting the sofa in place, I would try to cover it with the architectural color of the room—sky blue—so that it would fade into the background. I would use a sky-blue tweed or a sky-blue-and-white three-inch-wide stripe. Then I would add throw pillows of the floral fabric in the draperies plus some bright green and red throw pillows. I would then cover the two club chairs in delphinium blue and set them in front of a coffee table that could be period, such as French provincial, or white lacquer, or glass with a brass base. Then I would have a pull-up ottoman covered in bright red. I would add two lamps with shades done in a soft pink to give the room a glow. If the room were a studio and there were bedspreads and bedskirts to consider, I would use royal-blue skirts on the beds and choose a soft sky-blue spread and accent it again with the red and green pillows.

Most people are afraid to attempt this kind of look. Why? Because they can't see it with their color eye. They don't see how to combine every color of the rainbow and make it work. And so they begin to edit, and in the editing is where the full-force-color room falls apart in respect to color relationships.

I say, why not give it a try if you love the look of an old-fashioned flower garden? If you fail to be pleased, you can remove the offending colors as long as they are limited to accents like pillows or picture matting.

Color, Mood, and Environment

Casinos are usually green and red, because, like Christmas, they are associated with excitation, acquisitiveness, and even passion. Casino operators want to elicit all sorts of unconscious feelings of rampant desire and excitement. Red is an action color that makes you want to go out and get something. It's the predominant color you find in the body paint of primitive men going out to hunt. They literally want to create some red: make a killing. Casino operators have learned to saturate their environment with the colors that elicit the exact kind of response they're after: red for passion, green for money. What casino operators don't want is a peaceful blue environment where people are inclined to feel tranquil. They want an invigorating decor.

In airplane interiors there is rarely much use of strong, saturated colors. Rather, you will find blued-up colors in rust brown or turquoise. Airline interiors are designed to create an environment that is neutral to counteract some of the anxiety most people feel when they fly. People walking onto a plane are already in a heightened emotional state, and airline interior designers don't want to exaggerate those feelings. Instead, they want to eliminate all elements that will further stimulate the senses. The colors that would be perfect for a casino would be the worst colors inside an airplane.

There's a color in each of us that represents the mood in which we should like to live. How do we find that color? Even though you may not think you have found it, the colors you choose in the meantime present a mood to others that they pick up on. When I meet somebody for the first time, or observe the colors in a meal or a painting, I'm fascinated with what the colors of clothing, food, or paint communicate, sometimes unwittingly. If I go to a gallery show, I can learn a lot about an artist from the colors he or she works in. Many artists have color periods. Most of the paintings from that period will have a predominance of one color or a similar color feeling to them. The artist's color inspiration and the mood of the painting are intimately connected. In coloring your house, it's important to know your color mood. If you have your preferences definitely established, there's no decorator who can come in and tell you one room should be green, the other yellow, and a third red. You would resist such an idea, although I know decorators who will make such recommendations. I would call the house that is decorated that way a showcase disaster. Showcase houses that are used to sell products across the country rarely have a coordinated look from room to room, and I think that this is their main problem from a design point of view. You may go through a showcase house and see a coordination of style but a hodgepodge of colors. I respect the idea of doing showcases, especially for charity, but what usually happens is that one decorator comes in and does a modern room, another a traditional room, and the garret room will be done in high tech by a third, while the downstairs wicker room is done by a fourth. To me the end result is schizophrenia.

Do you have a mate or a mate-to-be in your life? Do the colors in your respective closets clash? If you really want an accurate idea about color preference, simply look at what people choose when they buy clothes. How much pink do you find in your closet? How much yellow or green? Men's shirts and ties are often good clues to their true color preferences, as are people's choices in bath towels. I think that people who get along best with each other wear colors that work well with each other, too. If the color tastes of mates range to the shockingly different I have often noted that their personalities clash as well.

For example, if you are someone who likes a soft-colored environment done in beiges, soft teal green, and a touch of coffee brown or old rose, can you really find happiness with someone who lives in a room with banana-yellow walls, a chartreuse ceiling, and fabrics of yellow, chartreuse, and black? The relationship between the person who likes shocking color combinations and the one who doesn't is going to be a problem, because the emotion that goes through the body of the soft-color person at the sight of all those strong colors will simply be too highly charged to enable him or her to live in peace.

Cosmetic Colors

There may be colors that are best for you simply for cosmetic reasons. It's a good idea to let your skin tone determine your preferences. You may say, "I can't wear a yellow shirt. I look all washed out." Some people can't wear specific colors because they don't feel good in them. They feel they don't look their best. I say, shun those colors. In even the most inexpensive items, there are colors that work for you and colors that work against you.

Orienting your color schemes to your own particular hair and skin coloring to make a pleasing cosmetic environment makes good sense to me. You may find you already have some prejudices against a group of colors because you have found over the years that they do not look good on you. But what particular colors *do* look good on you, and in what combinations, and in what shades? What colors should you avoid?

Cosmetic colors are divided into four basic types: *winter, spring, summer,* and *autumn.*

Winter people have a blue-based complexion. They often have black hair and blue or hazel eyes. Yves Saint Laurent colors are pure winter colors, as are the brilliant royal colors of purple and magenta. Even the warm colors are icy in the winter complexion. Winter people should avoid muddy colors, pastels, and the gold-toned colors of autumn. They don't look good in muted tones, but in clear, cool, brilliant ones. Winter jewelry is on the dramatic side. Avoid gold, and go for silver, platinum, and white gold. Black pearls and rhinestones are also enhancing to the winter person. Winter people often go salt-and-pepper gray. They are at their most attractive when they allow their hair to remain its natural color and avoid wearing the warmer tones.

Spring colors are those sunny bright colors that come with fresh growth: lime rather than deep summer green, peacock rather than royal blue. They are clear salmon and robin's egg, soft powder blue, light gray, mint green, clear apricot, and a bright red that is not too hot. There is a vividness to spring colors that is delicate at the same time. There are more colors in the spring palette than in any other, but there are none of the dark and muted shades. Spring people should avoid dark colors and all other extremes, including white and black. The blue-toned colors of winter aren't warm enough to enhance the skin and hair of the spring person, whose hair has warm tones in it of red or chestnut. There is a light golden cast to the hair as well as the complexion that fights the blue-toned colors and warms to the gentle ones. Spring jewelry should not be ornate but delicate like filigree. Yellow gold, opals, emeralds, and pearls all enhance the spring person.

Summer people are paler than spring folk. There might be a platinum or ash cast to their hair, and their skin is pink-toned. Summer people look good in the softer tones of pastels, the softer the more pleasing. Pink, powder blue, lavender, mauve, and the postmodern colors all enhance the summer group. Neutrals have a gray or beige cast to them. Dark colors are to be avoided, as is any color that is too intense or bright. Summer people should avoid a lot of contrast in their color combinations as well as black, white, and the orangey autumn shades. Summer jewelry is in the white range. Gold should be avoided, as well as large, chunky pieces. Clusters of stones are good in the soft colors that enhance the summer person's skin.

The autumn person is the one, who like winter, can really put on the full-color spectrum. Autumn glows, and so does the skin and hair of the autumn person whose complexion might have an olive cast, and whose hair might be a rich blue black or have red and gold highlights. Autumn people can take intense colors. In fact, they look stunning in them. There are all the rich, glowing autumn-leaf colors to choose from in addition to dark brown, brilliant green and blue, the olive and orange range of colors, and creamy white and caramel. Autumns should wear the warm colors in shades from light to dark, but they should avoid the pink-toned and the blue-toned colors as well as navy and black. Autumn jewelry is glowing gold in Baroque style. It's amber, topaz, jade, tortoiseshell, and pearls that are not too white but rather cream-colored. The kind of jewelry that sparkles in tiny clusters and that enhances the summer person should be avoided by the autumn person in favor of solid, large-scale jewelry.

In order to find your color group, you can be draped by a color consultant. In preparation for this book, I consulted Rosanna Ripamonti in Fort Lauderdale, Florida, where she has a color-consulting shop on Las Olas Boulevard. Rosanna draped my shoulders in bibs of the colors of the different seasons while I stood under a clear, bright light. The primary colors of red, blue, yellow, and green are used for the test, and there are four tones of each color, one representing each season. At the end of the draping, when each color has been applied to the chest and shoulders of the client, the colorist and the client have two piles. In one are the colors that flattered. In the other are the colors that did not. The winter colors are mixed with black for a vivid effect. Summer blue is a soft teal or azure blue in contrast to winter's royal blue. Winter-based green is blued and intense; summer green is almost in the peacock range. Autumn green is olive. Spring green is a yellow-based, electric kelly green.

Winter red is a deep cranberry. Summer doesn't really have a red but a magenta pink. Yellow-based red for autumn is a rich tomato red. For spring there is a similar red, but the color is clearer. Black as a color to wear is for winter people only. It is a very harsh color, more so than a lot of people realize. Most people look decapitated when they wear black: all you see is a head sticking out. There is no harmony between the colors in the face and hair and the stark black below. However, a person with strong coloring and blue-black glossy hair can wear black harmoniously. Black is the most blue-based of the colors. It tunes in perfectly with the winter person who has a blue-based skin and can take it, but it's too hard a color for any but winter people to carry.

Instead of black, summer people have silver brown, an unusual color with no gold in it, a salty desert color with a silver base. Autumn people have rich chocolate brown, and spring's equivalent is camel. Black is no color for hopeful spring. As for yellow, all the gold is stripped away in winter's and summer's yellows. Winter yellow is lemon, but it must not turn the blue-based person's skin that sickly shade that gold-based yellow gives them. It has to be as clear and pale as winter sunlight. Spring yellow is hot, clear, and delicate. It is the yellow of daffodils. Summer yellow is riper, closer to pineapple. Autumn's yellow is a deep mustard gold.

White is a color for the blue-based seasons of winter and summer, but spring and fall need to turn to a beiged-out cream. White brings out the pink tones in the skin of winter and summer people and makes them look healthy. But white washes out anybody with golden tones. It's such a harsh color and attracts so much light that it affects the golden-based complexion the same way gold-based yellows affect pink-based skin: it makes them look washed out and a bit sickly.

Metals can work for or against a person. Silver is for those with blue-based skin tones. Gold will make these people look jaundiced, especially around the jawline. But gold on those of the yellow-based seasons of spring and autumn gives a warm effect and brings out the golden glow in their skin.

If you choose colors outside of your cosmetic spectrum, they will drag you down. Look in a mirror with good light and see how holding up different colors to your complexion will play tricks or perform magic, depending on whether that color belongs to your season. The wrong color will turn you that color and make you look sallow. Shadows will appear where before there were none and everything above the color will seem to be pulled into it, which is why wearing the wrong color will literally "drag you down." The right colors lift and light up your face, they give you a glow.

If you are a summer person, as are many fair-skinned people, then the yellow-based autumn colors are not for you. They will make you look jaundiced and sallow. Electric spring colors do not harmonize with your skin either. They're too bright for you and create too much of a contrast with your complexion. Winter colors are much too harsh and vivid. Summer colors, however, are just right. Surround yourself with them and everything falls into place.

Winter people look best with icy tones in their surroundings. For instance, they could paint their walls an icy pink that is almost a white. Summer people often decorate with winter-based colors. Although they can't wear these vivid colors, they like to surround themselves with them, for the lack of yellow in winter colors appeals to their taste. Summer people like Oriental carpets because they are often in winter-based colors, blue-based without any yellow. If summer people opt for summer colors in their home decor, they could paint their walls a light Wedgwood blue, a color that is flattering to them. The autumn person might opt for beige, but also for cinnamon, taupe, sable, copper, coral, salmon, and a yellow-based tomato red. In the yellow-loving autumn person there is a wide selection of decorating colors in goldenrod yellow, rust, saffron, hunter green, deep sage, and pumpkin orange.

If your complexion falls into the winter category, there are many ways to make your room flattering to you. You are someone who could live with shocking-pink walls and bright purple accents. You might also like to live with cranberry, and could choose a black and royal blue polka-dot fabric. When it comes to green, there are two greens you particularly like, one jungle and the other kelly. You might also like a pale teal green for summer sheets. Your color for jewelry is silver. You might consider doing a room in a combination of turquoise and silver.

If you are a winter person, here is a color scheme for your bedroom that would work for you. Paint your walls a soft aqua blue. Make sure that the blue has no yellow in it. Accent the walls with a soft banana cream. For a print at your windows, pick a fabric with a pine-green background highlighted with colors of soft aquamarine blue, pale winter-sun yellow, and maybe a dash of rich magenta. Magenta against green with an accent of aqua and white can be a very flattering winter combination.

For your carpet, pick the softest leaf green you can find, one that is close to the color of the background of your draperies. For an accent piece, pick deep bottle-green velvet to cover a long chaise. When thinking about bed treatments, consider a print with the teal-green background for the skirt, and for sheets, pick the softest aqua you can find. If you like, you could even paint the ceiling aquamarine so that you could dream you are sleeping under a Mediterranean sky.

Silver and mirrored items make this room work. I would pick white furniture with a soft blue trim because brown is really not a color in your spectrum. Or, why not pick black lacquered furniture? It would be striking against the aquamarine walls. Add mirrors at either side of the bed to create a look in harmony with every aspect of you.

Spring people like orange, melon, pale kumquat, peach, beige, and the brightest red. They also look good in azalea, a soft salmon, and a rich tan. In the green family, they like kelly green, citrus green, and bright mint green as well as turquoise. Spring people like to live with soft lilac in the blue tones as well as the deeper tones. Spring wears Wedgwood blue. Gold is the color of their jewelry. Spring yellows go from canary to banana to soft yellow. Spring complexions look good in brown, taupe, beige, camel, and rust. The white spectrum is also for the spring person, but with just a hint of beige in it.

The colors of the Far East are right for the spring person: purple, peach, saffron, orange, bright citrus green, and turquoise. Here's an Oriental-style spring scheme that you could try in your bedroom. Paint all your walls azalea. For a print, pick a Bangkok silk that combines red, orange, azalea, bright green, and turquoise. I know that sounds like a hard combination of colors to find, but those colors are readily available together in Thai silk, and they have a golden glow to them that puts them in the spring color spectrum. I would use this fabric for the draperies, hung on poles that have been painted gold, and for the skirts of the bed. If the bedcovers were azalea like the walls, it would help shrink the size of the bed.

Here is an idea for a room in postmodern colors for the summer person, who looks good in those grayed-down tones. Begin with walls of grayed heather. With them use a flannel-gray carpet and at the windows hang a print of grayed heather and white on fabric-covered poles. Paint the furniture soft heather with a high-gloss lacquer finish. For accessories, use Art Deco lamps.

Deep mint green, especially when it's frosted, fits in magically to the postmodern room. Summer people look good in beige or surrounded by the softest of the pinks. They can also choose from the spectrum of luscious blue greens, from teal to rich aqua, and all the water greens, but not the pure greens, and never a red. A mint-green dining room for a summer person might have chairs with gray-painted frames and seats covered in a pale magenta fabric. On the floor could be a gray carpet with a grape and magenta border. For placemats, I would use gray linen with white trim to offset gleaming magenta-colored postmodern-style dishes. The centerpiece might be modern Scandinavian in feeling and could contain silver candlesticks such as those made by Georg Jensen. It might also include a silver bowl filled with cymbidia. These orchids have the post-modern tones that appeal so much to the summer person with a pink-toned skin.

The male of the summer spectrum looks good in navy-blue pinstripes. He could wear a soft pink-to-mauve-colored shirt and for a tie might choose navy with a touch of blue and soft mauve in the design. Such a man's apartment might include the same combination of color and fabric. I would paint the walls navy and cover the sofa in a suiting material like a navy and white pinstripe. I would accent the sofa with light gray and gray-mauve pillows. Of course, all this gray requires a lot of contrast from the lighting and accessories. The artwork would have to be full of life. For example, one could choose a seascape with rich blued-out greens of peacock and aqua, which would be an interesting canvas against those navy-blue walls. Also, accessories could provide a dash of burgundy in the room.

The autumn person can take stronger, darker colors than the summer person, but these colors are not as alive and vivid. His or her complexion is golden-hued or olive. The autumn person looks good in the sunlit colors of fall: cranberry, rust, bright red, fir tree, salmon, goldenrod, beige, blue green, and turquoise. Most of all the autumn person likes gold. If I were to decorate a room for an autumn person I would begin with blue-green walls. For the sofa I would pick a large, beautiful paisley in blue green, dark green, red, soft fawn, and a lot of coffee brown. For the carpet I would use a rich beige tweed, because autumn has a tweedy look. There could be two chairs in the room covered in a fawn beige, preferably in leather. The same paisley print as on the sofa could be used at the windows, and for a snappy touch the drapes could be lined in golden yellow. We could pick up that yellow and add tomato red as accents in the room. For instance, we might use a bright red lacquered coffee table to highlight the touch of red in the paisley print. Or, for something more subtle, we might paint that coffee table a deep marine blue.

This room calls for jewelry in the brassy tones. Lamps could be of the big turned-brass variety with beige shades trimmed in marine blue. One of the things this room could also use for fun, because it is on the dark side, is a hassock covered in a deep cordovan leather. For this room, I would also recommend the colors of an English hunting painting hung over the sofa.

Another scheme for the person who likes autumn colors is to do a whole room in rust. Here we could use rust-colored walls with rust, beige, and cordovan in a geometric plaid carpet. Or we could cover the sofa in a rust suede and accent it with cordovan and rich burnt-orange pillows. Window shutters could also be burnt orange. Here again we would need the color of brass to liven up the room. A hostess in this room would look smashing in a gold lamé fabric.

Local Color

Over the years I have designed many hotels, each an environment in which people live only temporarily. I have received numerous letters from people who write, "I felt so good in that room" or "I felt terrible in that room!" If I go to a hotel, tired from a long trip, and walk into a room that is colored in a manner I find abrasive, I'll ask to be moved to another. Of course, what's abrasive for me may not be abrasive for another person. If, for instance, I am given a room done in a lot of postmodern colors, those trendy gray-rose rooms with gray-rose carpet and gray-rose chests of drawers, I feel depressed. To me it's a nothing room in a nothing color. After arriving in a place like Singapore, having crossed oceans and continents by plane, my eyes need a jolt. After all those hours in a cooled-out airplane interior, I want to have a room that looks alive, because I feel so dead. I want to see red, or a strong-colored wall in yellow, or a yellow carpet, or a yellow-and-white-striped fabric at the windows. I need something around me that will help me to feel fresh again.

I think my own attitude is one of the reasons that my hotel rooms have been so successful. I do give people who take a trip a sense of freshness when they arrive at their room. Of course, I don't do hotels the same way I do houses, because people stay in hotels for only a short period of time. Hotel rooms are not rooms to live *with* but live *in* and they should give you a strong sense of place. I always do my hotel rooms environmentally, that is, I bring the colors of the city or country itself inside. If I were to do a room in Honolulu, for example, I would try to use Hawaiian colors. I might use orchid walls with white trim, put down a jungle-green carpet, use white, orchid, and green floral fabric prints, and bring in a white planter holding great big tropical ferns.

When I work in different cities around the world I am always aware of the light factor. In Ireland there is a unique long-lived light in summer. The sun comes up early and sets late and it can be light until ten-thirty at night. I take into account this clarity of light in the colors I choose there. I have found that I can use the garden colors in Ireland to good effect. People usually use neutral or natural colors when decorating in an Irish style, but I like to use pretty melons, soft pinks, and rose.

If I were to do a room in downtown Cincinnati, I would try to do things in colors related to the neutrals: my favorite sky blue with accents of beige and brown. I might use sky-blue walls and carpet, traditional English furniture, bedspreads in sky blue and beige, and black lacquer or big blue-and-white Chinese porcelain lamps. That's my idea of a city-related room.

Color-preference tests of westerners show that they really do prefer those bright, sun-drenched desert-flower colors, perhaps because color has to make a big statement to leave any kind of impression on the Western landscape. I believe that the sun of the Southwest is meant to shine on those bright, vivid desert colors, and I like to see them used as accents in an earth-colored Southwestern home with adobe walls. If I were to do a hotel room in Arizona, as I actually have, I would select Navaho colors: clay-colored walls and carpet, beige wovens on the sofas, sun-yellow side chairs, and sun-yellow and orange accessories.

If I were to do a room in the Caribbean, I might use hibiscus pink for the walls, white trim, and natural rattan furniture. If I were to do a room in the state of Washington, and if that room were large, I might carry inside all those rich, dark forest greens of the Northwest and use a lot of pictures of local scenery. I have never been able to understand public places where unrelated environmental scenes are hung on the wall. For example, I remember once being in a hotel in Seattle and finding pictures on the wall of New York. Were they trying to make me feel at home? I don't know, but the effort is misguided, because every environment has its own special beauty. I always try to highlight that special beauty in the colors I choose and the accessories and paintings that I use.

When I work with a particular environment, I begin by looking for a color idea that is compatible with the local scene.

I do design work all over the world, and have found that no two places are alike. What will work in one place will not necessarily work in another. I always like to create a mood that is regional in feeling. For example, the mood of the Southwest is determined by the dry terrain. The mood of the Caribbean is determined by the softness of the air, the openness of the island atmosphere, and the ever-present jungle. However, I don't think you can move that jungle look into downtown Chicago or Minneapolis. It just won't work. I would no sooner do a room with a tropical-island feeling to it in Detroit than I would do a hearty British-tweed look in Aruba.

When I do a house in the islands, it has to have a cool feeling about it. In a room with dark jungle-green walls I would use natural wicker furniture, which would give an impression of palm trees. For upholstery I would select a dark green like the walls. There's a serenity about this color scheme that reflects its environment. Because the nature of the earth is clay-like and sunbaked in these places, I like a baked-looking tile floor that has a sun-bleached terra-cotta feeling to it. I like an area rug in cotton on those tiles as well, something you can pick up and wash. I also like the look of a natural-colored fly fan against a dark green ceiling and clay pots holding leafy jungle plants lit from below.

If you were to add a modern look to that terra-cotta and natural wicker environment, you would run the risk of destroying the mood you have created. If you filled the room with steel and glass objects that are contemporary and citylike, the room wouldn't work. In a major metropolis where they fit right in there's no problem with ultramodern accessories, but they don't belong in the tropics.

Unfortunately, because of the economics of construction today, the steel and glass world *has* moved to the tropics where it appears as the condo on the beach. What happens when people move from a northern city to a place like San Juan, Escondido, Miami, or Tampa is that they paint the walls gray and put down their burgundy carpet from Minneapolis. They also bring down the dove-gray sofa with the burgundy pillows, the glass coffee table with the steel base, and the lamps made of chrome with white shades. Then they put modern vertical blinds in the sliding glass window. Closing the blinds, they sit back in their tropical paradise and turn on the air conditioner thinking they have transported themselves. Ironically, the gray-flannel look works only *because* the air-conditioning is on.

Shocks of color out of doors are also environmentally abrasive. I find it unappealing to see beach chairs of purple webbing with black frames or turquoise webbing with orange frames on the sand. Even a rust color bothers me there. I feel beach chairs, traditional or modern, should be the color of sand or in the classic awning stripe. If not, they jump out at you. In nature's own beautiful setting, I think it's poor manners to draw needless attention to the human-made thing.

Whether indoors or out, colors that jump out at you don't work, it's as simple as that. If you are in doubt about what color sofa you should have, cover it in the same color as your walls and it will recede in a pleasing way. But if you put a red sofa against a gray wall, or a chartreuse sofa against a yellow wall, or a lavender sofa against a red wall, those sofas might very well take a flying leap at you. What should stand out in a room should never be the architecture, by which I mean the walls, carpeting, and larger pieces of upholstery. The things that stand out in a room should be the personal things, the things that are one-of-a-kind. The people in the room should stand out—framed, mirrored, and attractively lighted. Or the beautiful Chinese lamp brought back from the Orient should stand out. Something that is handmade with artistry should stand out. If you follow this rule, you will have an environment that is both tranquil and stimulating at the same time.

Most of all, consider what you want your environment to

say and mean. How do you envision the atmosphere of your home? Do you use your home to rest in, to relax and feel comfortable in? Generally most people do, but some people use their environments as showplaces, or as after-hours entertainment spots with an electrifying atmosphere that contrasts with the doldrums of their office environment. A person who lives a very active life may want to come home to something more restful than the person who has just spent the day in the accounting department. This need for contrast in environment is also true in my own life. While I advocate the use of a great deal of color, being around it all the time in my work, I find I have to have a certain kind of color serenity at home, particularly in the city. There I need a played-down feeling. I have to rest my color sensors. Yet, in the country, where I am away from all the decision making about color, I find I can live with a great deal of color. So I think that, above all, one should consider one's own need for color contrast when planning the home environment.

How to Change Colors

When people decide to change color in their homes, it can be traumatic. They wonder for weeks whether they could live in a blue or red or green room. They are reluctant to make a mistake. Many people choose to avoid mistakes altogether by opting for what I call *vanilla decorating*. They are people who could be presented with thirty-six varieties, but every time they go for vanilla.

Many more people want to change their decorating colors but don't know how. For them, choosing color in paint, fabric, and accessories becomes a dilemma. But the dilemma in decorating *is* color itself. Decorating isn't so much about furniture or about the kind of draperies you hang. It isn't about what's "in" and what's "out." It's about the colors in combination that you, the home decorator, put together.

When you begin to have a sense of a master plan, the marriage of your favorite colors, you also need to be aware of the practical side of color in home decorating. You need to know what things need redoing relatively soon. Paint has to be redone every few years. In New York City for instance, the law provides that tenants shall have a paint job every three years. Light, dirt, humidity, and general wear and tear all affect paint. In order to maintain a feeling of freshness, you have to be able to keep your surfaces bright. I think it's a good idea to plan a color change each time you paint your home. Between time, you can dream about color.

I have always believed I could take a plain standard studio apartment and for under two thousand dollars transform that white featureless room into something magical. How? With color, of course. Envision a small, one-room studio apartment. If it were a woman's apartment, I might paint the ceiling in stripes of soft pink and white to look like a tent. This can be done easily with mastic tape and brown paper. If the ceiling is already white, cut out strips three inches wide and tape them to the ceiling. Then spray the entire ceiling pink. Remove the brown paper and mastic and you have your pink-and-white tented ceiling. That kind of color magic takes a little work on your part, but it also begins to show you what color can do just on the ceiling for the cost of a gallon or two of paint.

When it comes to refurbishing the rest of the room on this limited budget, I would paint all the interiors of the closets the same color as the pink in the ceiling, and the walls white. If the floor was not in good shape, I would paint it green if the lease allowed. If it was in good shape, or if it was not permitted to paint the floor because the lease required carpeting on certain portions of the floor, then I would put down a green carpet in a fresh green shade, as close to green grass as possible. On a shoestring budget there wouldn't be room for wall-to-wall carpeting, but it might be possible to find a moderately priced nylon carpet on sale that would be just right.

I would then begin to fill the room with interesting pieces of furniture in white wicker. I would choose a pink fabric for the cushions and a small green and white ticking stripe for the throw pillows. At the windows I would use pink shades with decorative pulls. If there were white shades in place, they could be painted pink using a latex paint made especially to adhere to such surfaces. Modern furniture also fits in well with this color scheme. A good choice might be all-white in the easy-to-care-for, inexpensive, and popular laminate. Cubes of laminate could be used for coffee and end tables. Inexpensive lamps could be made by taking an old lamp and giving it a new base by tie-dyeing a white pillowcase pink and white. Then the pillowcase should be stiffly starched. The old lamp whose base is being covered is slipped into the starched pillowcase and the pillowcase is tied at the top of the base with a pink bow. For a shade, an inexpensive accordian-pleated one is a good choice. In this way, for next to nothing, a tired old lamp is given a new look.

From this example, you can see that to create environmental magic, the one essential element is color. I could redo that studio room and never change the furniture, only the color, and transform the mood. For example, I'm often told by people living in studio apartments, "I have a beige sofa, beige draperies, and have covered my dining-room chairs in beige to match my beige carpet." These people want to know "What can I do?"

In fact, you can do almost anything, including painting the walls bright lacquer red. I know that's going too far for most people, so I make the next boldest statement I can and suggest they paint the walls gold, the trim cream, and the ceiling white.

I advise them to add some touches of blue and gold to their sofas. Although this color choice is bold, it's not shocking.

Let's say you dare to go with the bright red walls, however. In that case, I would stain the floors a dark, teak brown black. With that combination of color, you can begin to bring in Oriental decor with furniture that is black or red lacquer. Rattan furniture also would be a good choice. A wonderful Oriental screen could frame the room, making a major artistic statement.

You can bring to that scarlet-walled room an English look by adding a Chippendale sofa covered in beige damask with red velvet pillows and Queen Anne pull-up chairs upholstered in a red, white, and beige stripe.

Or you could give that red studio room a "down-home" look. Choose a sofa covered in a beige-and-white tweed; hang a multicolored Star of Bethlehem patchwork quilt in predominating colors of red and white on the wall; choose interesting old apothecary jars for lamps, and bring in country hunt tables.

Red is one of those colors that gives vibrancy to an environment. Many people think otherwise. For example, they believe that when you paint a room a dark or a strong color that makes it seem smaller than it really is. I disagree. Over the years I have found that whether a room is painted red or beige or yellow or white or blue, it's going to appear to be about the same size. You can't elasticize rooms. That's decorator mumbo-jumbo. People have been led to believe that color can make a room look drastically bigger or smaller, but it really can't.

Although it may sound strange, I don't really believe in the concept of *redecorating*. Rather, I believe in keeping things in good condition all the time. A home environment requires constant maintenance, like your teeth or complexion or wardrobe. A house is never complete. It can't be the same tomorrow as it was yesterday. The candles burn down. The upholstery fades. The frames of the chairs begin to weaken. Fortunately, some things don't get old but just get better, like some people. There's something about a well-used object that has developed character through the passage of time, such as a favorite old robe that you can't throw away. There's a certain "warmth" to these objects, and I don't believe in eliminating them or replacing them unless it is aesthetically necessary. Sometimes reupholstering an old piece takes away a special quality or feeling. The fabric will be too new and out of keeping with the wood in the piece or with the other things around it in the room. Don't forget to take into consideration your aging patinas as you contemplate color changes.

Another thing that happens during color change is that other objects in a room that aren't changed may suddenly look quite dreary and shabby. Paint your walls and you may soon be motivated to give your upholstered pieces new slipcovers. I remember an old Thurber cartoon where the lady of the house critically regards her slovenly husband who sits in the middle of her freshly decorated room. Changing color doesn't necessarily lead to a change in housemates, but it does tend to be a matter of one change leading to another. So be prepared.

Color Styles

Now that you're familiar with the properties of color, what of color itself? What is it made of? Since the beginning of art, color has been made of materials that were of the earth, whether animal, vegetable, or mineral. The custom did not change until the middle of the last century when the era of chemical-color was born. Until then, people colored their homes and their clothes with a wide variety of natural pigments and dyes. Of course, that variety was nothing like the color glut that came after the birth of the chemical color industry, but it may have been more to your liking.

Today, with the exception of the postmodernists, most people have returned to the colors that are of the earth rather than of the chemical dye pot. Of course, if a chemical color looks like the real thing, so much the better, for the great advantage of today's coloring materials is their stability. For centuries people who could afford its high cost wanted vermilion in their paintings and frescoes. However, vermilion, costly as it was, could turn black overnight. Imagine the consternation of seeing the fresco that you paid a fortune for because of its lavish use of vermilion suddenly lose its red color. If you buy a color today, you don't have to worry about its instability. Nor do you usually have to worry about fading, unless you want that look, in which case you can buy fibers prefaded for your convenience.

So we have the best of both worlds in terms of color. Color looks its best, I believe, when applied to natural materials like wool, cotton, and linen. You can use a modern colorfast dye on these natural products and enjoy the best of the present and the past. Of course, there's not much lapis lazuli around in wall coloring even for the most affluent today, although that precious mineral was once ground to a powder, mixed with an oil, and applied to surfaces as sparkling ultramarine. But other than the lack of the truly ultimate colors of the past, we have little to complain of.

There are two major categories of coloring materials: dye and pigment. *Dyes* dissolve in a solvent and are most commonly used on fibers. Because the color dissolves in the solvent, like granules of gelatin dessert immersed in boiling water, the dye can penetrate the material such as fabric or paper when it is dipped into the solvent. The result can be a clear, almost translucent, color. Dyes have been used on fibers for at least 3,000 years, and although color choice was fairly limited until the last century, the way in which fibers were dyed also did not change much over the centuries. Now and then traders or explorers would bring back a new color like Tyrian purple or Aztec red. These exotic colors would then become vastly popular among those who could afford the high price and coveted by those who could not. Until the nineteenth century, the wearing of bright colors or living with them in homes was limited to the upper classes. Everyone else went to church to enjoy the stained-glass windows for man-made color in their lives.

The other way to use color is as a *pigment*. Unlike dyes, pigments do not penetrate. They lie on top of the object. Unlike the powdered dye product that dissolves in its medium, the pigment powder is suspended in a medium, such as oil, and is much thicker than the dye solvent. The first man-made pigments were mineral-based, and there were few colors to choose from. Ochre, or natural earth color, produced red, which was used in the burial rites of Neanderthal man. Ochre also produced yellow and brown. A reddish brown was made from hematite, a bluish color from manganese, a black and dark brown from an oxide of manganese, and a violet was most likely derived from a magniferous mineral. We also find evidence that human beings near the end of the Ice Age colored their world with vegetable colors made from crushed roots, berries, and leaves. Surely the first red fabric came from someone rubbing the juice of a ripe berry onto woven material and observing with pleasure the new color.

It is possible to see the complete color chart available to artists of early times in the prehistoric cave paintings in Spain and France. These are colors that will be found on any painter's palette today. It's amazing how the mineral colors of the earth, in all their rich variety and splendor, continue to be favorites, year in and year out. The colors we see in the caves, yellow and red ochres, Venetian red, Indian red, raw and burnt sienna, and umber, are made from clay that contains iron compounds. With this limited color scheme, together with white chalk, the prehistoric artists of the caves created wall coverings of great beauty and mystery, featuring galloping animals, spotted unicorns, sticklike human figures, palm prints, and mysterious geometrics, all with a highly sophisticated fluidity of design. These caves are among the greatest of our human treasures.

A study done on the early stages of the development of language in various cultures around the world found that in the beginning there were very few names for colors after black and white. Red is usually the first color to be given a name, followed by yellow, green, and blue. In the Bible, the first mention of color, after the brief note about Esau being red and hairy at birth, is in Exodus 26:31. The passage gives instructions for the manner in which the tabernacle should be decorated. "And thou shalt make a veil of blue, and purple, and scarlet, and fine twined linen of cunning work with cherubims shall it be made. And thou shalt hang it upon four pillars of shittim wood overlaid in gold . . ."

Where did the artists who decorated the tabernacle get their coloring materials? The ancients had a limited repertoire of dyes before they took to the sea in large boats or traded long distances overland by horse and camel. In a desert there would have been madder root for a subdued red, green from elder leaves, and yellow from tree sap, but the source of bright blue and deep purple came from India and was called indigo. When trade was opened to and from the Far East, the Holy Land was on the route, and indigo was a popular import. It would have provided the dense and brilliant blue and purple colors that are mentioned so often in the Bible.

Yet, in the desert there are enough colorants to produce a coat of many colors. The coloring materials for the special religious cloths of purple and scarlet mentioned in Exodus were probably the best available and an artisan's trade secret. The process by which colors were made, especially those coveted brilliant colors, was always a well-kept secret. So well were some of these secrets kept that they have been lost to history. Nobody knows, for instance, how medieval stained-glass window-makers produced their brilliant colors. Like the great chefs, the great colorists had their closely guarded recipes.

"How do you *get* that color?" I once heard someone ask a painter friend of mine who I knew didn't like to give away such information.

"Just mix around," he said.

Homer's use of color in the *Odyssey* has confused and perplexed people for centuries. Anyone who has seen the limpid blue, sunlit waters of the Aegean would never describe them as wine-dark, as Homer does. All sorts of theories have been advanced, including one that the acid in the metal of ancient wine goblets turned the wine copper blue! But whatever the solution, there's just no getting around the fact that the seas crossed by Odysseus are brilliant blue and not dark. This confusion about color is not at all surprising. It just shows how little there was in the way of standardized colors until the nineteenth century.

Cinnabar red was the first brilliant red pigment of the ancient world. Until the discovery of vermilion, made from compounds of mercury and sulfur, the most treasured source of the highly coveted scarlet, worn only by the upper classes of ancient times, came from liver-colored pebbles found in the bottom of the mineral-rich Minium river in Spain. The cost of cinnabar was astronomical. The historian Pliny describes how the Romans jealously guarded the monopoly on the cinnabar trade. "Nothing is more carefully guarded. It is forbidden to break up or refine the cinnabar on the spot. They send it to Rome in its natural color, under seal, to the extent of some ten thousand pounds a year."

Of course, there were knock-off reds for the *hoi polloi*. The root of the madder plant had been used since ancient times to produce a red dye, but no root gives a sun-bright red. There was dragon's-blood red, made from a red resin, that approached the color of the coveted cinnabar. But until the third century b.c., when mercury and sulfur were combined to make vermilion, the rare cinnabar was the only source of scarlet in the ancient world. Vermilion was not the ideal substitute either, because of its propensity to turn black when exposed to air and sunlight.

In color history, true bright red has always been derived from rare and costly sources. All through the Middle Ages vermilion was more costly even than ultramarine, which was made from crushed lapis lazuli. All that changed, of course, in the middle of the last century. With the cornucopia of color brought by the chemical industry, red eventually became cheapened. The social status of red has been reversed in the modern age.

Another brilliant and, therefore, precious color of ancient times was yellow. Imagine the surprise of Europeans when they saw their first garment dipped in saffron, that powerful concentration of the sunny spectrum. Saffron comes from the dried stigmas of a brilliant purple crocus native to the Far East. Another name for saffron is vegetable gold. Saffron is light in weight, an essential requirement in overland trade during all those long centuries before the advent of sea trade. Its costli-

A kitchen in red with strawberry motifs (see page 5).

A skipper-blue bathroom (see pages 7–8).

A yellow island-living dining room (see pages 11–12).

A grass-green English-style living room in Southampton, Long Island (see page 17).

Dorothy Draper's purple living room (see pages 19–20).

A fire-orange Oriental living room (see pages 24–25).

A black postmodern bedroom (see pages 29–30).

A white living room in the Continental style (see page 23).

A brown and pastel traditional bedroom (see page 35).

A full-force-color room (see pages 58–59).

A winter-based bedroom in cosmetic colors (see page 67).

An Englishman's library in Rolls-Royce green (see page 95 and English color wheel).

A French bedroom in yellow (see pages 97–98 and French color wheel).

An Italian dining room in terra rosa (see pages 98–99 and Italian color wheel).

An Oriental room in Thai silk colors (see pages 101–102 and Oriental color wheel).

A green Americana living room (see page 105 and Americana color wheel).

A slate-blue Colonial living room (see pages 106–107 and Colonial color wheel).

A pink and white room in Bermuda (see page 110 and island-living color wheel).

A gray postmodern living room (see page 119 and postmodern color wheel).

A 1950s-style New York apartment (see pages 120–121 and American-modern color wheel).

A Southwestern living room in Georgia O'Keeffe colors (see pages 135–136).

A vermilion dining room (see page 140).

A yellow Oriental dining room (see page 142).

A color-coded child's room in primary colors (see pages 150–151).

A Colonial blue boy's room (see pages 151–152).

An American-modern bedroom in primary colors (see pages 154–155).

A pastel country-style bedroom (see page 155).

A bathroom in autumn-based colors (see page 158).

A raspberry bathroom in the French manner (see pages 158–159).

ENGLISH COLOR WHEEL

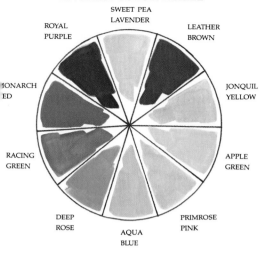

ROYAL PURPLE
SWEET PEA LAVENDER
LEATHER BROWN
MONARCH RED
JONQUIL YELLOW
RACING GREEN
APPLE GREEN
DEEP ROSE
AQUA BLUE
PRIMROSE PINK

FRENCH COLOR WHEEL

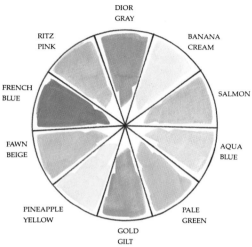

DIOR GRAY
RITZ PINK
BANANA CREAM
FRENCH BLUE
SALMON
FAWN BEIGE
AQUA BLUE
PINEAPPLE YELLOW
PALE GREEN
GOLD GILT

ITALIAN COLOR WHEEL

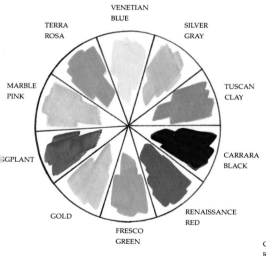

VENETIAN BLUE
TERRA ROSA
SILVER GRAY
MARBLE PINK
TUSCAN CLAY
EGGPLANT
CARRARA BLACK
GOLD
RENAISSANCE RED
FRESCO GREEN

ORIENTAL COLOR WHEEL

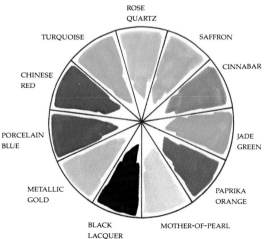

ROSE QUARTZ
TURQUOISE
SAFFRON
CHINESE RED
CINNABAR
PORCELAIN BLUE
JADE GREEN
METALLIC GOLD
PAPRIKA ORANGE
BLACK LACQUER
MOTHER-OF-PEARL

AMERICANA COLOR WHEEL

INDIGO
BLUE

SUMMER
GREEN

BARN
RED

TOBACCO

WHEAT

MADDER
RED

MUSTARD

DUSKY
GRAY

BUTTERCUP
YELLOW

SPRING
GREEN

COLONIAL COLOR WHEEL

WHITEWASH
WHITE

INDIGO
VIOLET

SLATE
BLUE

INDIGO
BLUE

GOLDEN
YELLOW

PEWTER
GRAY

FAWN
BEIGE

BARN
RED

BOXWOOD
GREEN

TREEN
GREEN

ISLAND-LIVING COLOR WHEEL

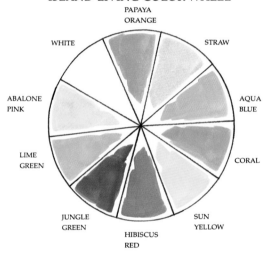

PAPAYA
ORANGE

WHITE

STRAW

ABALONE
PINK

AQUA
BLUE

LIME
GREEN

CORAL

JUNGLE
GREEN

SUN
YELLOW

HIBISCUS
RED

POSTMODERN COLOR WHEEL

GREIGE

DEAD
WHITE

HEATHER

SLATE
BLACK

CLARET

DUSTY
RASPBERRY

FLANNEL
GRAY

AMBER
ORANGE

DUSTY
ROSE

WATERED
AQUAMARINE

AMERICAN MODERN COLOR WHEEL

ROYAL
BLUE

RASPBERRY

WHITE

ORANGE

BRIG
RED

MAGENTA

YELLO

BLACK

BRIGHT
GREEN

TURQUOISE

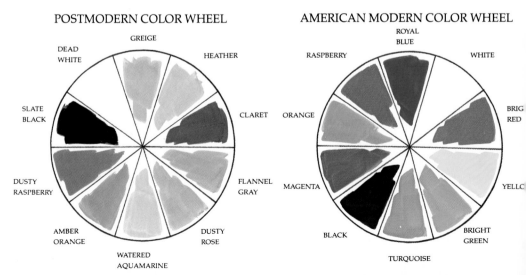

ness was derived from the difficulty of harvesting it and the long distances it had to be transported across deserts and mountains.

In the East, of course, saffron is used lavishly. I have seen pictures of whole hillsides of Eastern religious men in saffron robes. In the ancient West, however, saffron was a treasure, accumulation of which, like gold, meant status and power.

The third brilliant color of ancient times was blue. It was a dye that came from the Far East, the best quality from India. Like saffron, indigo was a product that could be transported by camel or horse by way of the great overland trade routes to and from the East. Indigo was a highly prized color of ancient Egypt, Greece, and Rome. The indigo plant was chopped up, mixed with water, and allowed to rot and dry in the sun until it formed a paste. The brighter and richer the color it yielded, the higher the price. Like saffron, indigo was part of the trade that brought to the less-developed West the highly sophisticated art and adornment of the East.

There were local western substitutes for this costly import. Woad, for example, is a common European plant that will yield a serviceable blue, but it lacks the fading properties of indigo, which improves with age and use.

The continued popularity of indigo today can be seen in denim, a fabric that is coveted the world over. Modern blue-jean fabric fades in a clever way. Jean denim is made with a warp of indigo. These are the threads that show on the surface of the fabric. Then the warp is woven with a white weft. This is the underthread that when exposed through wear will give the desired faded-blue quality that is impossible to achieve by regular dying. Making indigo colorfast in ancient times was an expensive process. Making it fade is equally expensive today. When you buy that prewashed color in brand-new jeans, you're paying for the fading process along with the designer name.

Royal purple was the fourth and most precious color of ancient times. It was the purple of Byzantium, of emperors. Purple is also associated with the colors of the sea, and therefore it should be no surprise that royal purple dye comes from the sea, from the tiny rare murex shellfish. Murex purple was made from millions of the mollusks, each of which yielded a tiny drop of fluid. This was then mixed with white earth and the resulting pigments had a wide range of shades, from blue black to plum to lavender.

If we look at the colors of medieval art, the first thing we will note is their brightness and jewellike brilliance. Imagine how much more brilliant they were hundreds of years ago! The medieval palette, like the medieval palate, was characterized by an appetite for plenty of rich, robust fare in great abundance.

The colors of the art of the Middle Ages remain astonishingly clear and bright to this day. In that age of early scientific discovery, the color palette was expanded and stabilized. Through alchemy, the forerunner of chemistry, many new exciting colors were born. New pigments were derived from the artificial combination of various minerals as well as from gems and were far more stable and less likely to fade than those made from natural plant-derived dyes. One of these new colors was cadmium, a versatile yellow made from a mineral that could vary from pale, clear yellow to orange, opening up a whole new color range.

One exception to the rule of not sharing color recipes was a book written by a Renaissance craftsman from Florence, Cennino d'Andrea Cennini. He recorded all his trade secrets in *The Craftsman's Handbook* (c. 1437; reprint, New York: Dover Publications, 1960) and included everything known about color up to that time. Step by step, the master instructed the uninitiated in exactly how he laboriously worked up his celestial colors in order to achieve those stunning, vivid, and light-filled Renaissance colors. The book gives detailed instructions, and reading about the grinding, measuring, sifting, kneading, and scraping that had to be done, one begins to understand what color meant before the nineteenth century. Until the advent of the chemical industry, making color was a difficult, complicated, dangerous, and arduous muscular activity.

The most plentiful source of medieval red continued to come from iron-rich minerals. The craftsman Cennini was fond of locating seams of "sinoper" red in the earth of his native Italy because the color, a light vermilion shade, worked up well and could be used both in and out of doors. Red ochre is still called Sinopia today. You will find it on most painter's palettes and even on the color sticks at your house-paint store. But the medieval painter had more than Sinopia to rely on. There was also light and warm Venetian red, cold and dark Indian red, and clear salmon pink from the clay of Naples called terra rosa. Blood red continued to be made from the mineral hematite and still can be seen in the frescoes of Florence, the hometown of the craftsman Cennini. Vermilion is the rich, ripe red so favored by medieval painters. Because vermilion would turn black when exposed to air and sunlight, it was used more in paintings than in frescoes. There was also cardinal red made from bloodstone. Dragon's-blood red was used as ink for parchment, being a dye rather than a pigment. It could no longer compete with the brilliance of the mineral pigments. Not all strongly red minerals produce red pigment, however. If one were extravagant enough to pound a ruby to powder, one would end up with a pile of worthless white dust.

Ultramarine blue has been described by Cennini as "perfect beyond all other colors." I, too, feel that way about the right ultramarine blue. The emphasis, of course, must be on the *ultra* or else one ends up with a disappointing turquoise. Ultramarine is an ocean color, a mixture of green and blue like the Gulf Stream. It is said that you can see the Gulf Stream from the air as a vein of flowing green water in the surrounding blue. Ultramarine is the commingling of blue and green, a flowing, sensuous, and light-filled color without a hint of yellow, although with a slight violet cast.

Italian artisans made ultramarine out of lapis lazuli, which is a color of blue in its mineral state to make you faint. Lapis lazuli is pure brilliant blue-blueness, as true blue a color as you can get. The richest-colored lapis lazuli crystals were ground to a powder, sifted, and then made into a paste with the addition of melted wax, pine resin, gum mastic, and linseed oil. It must have been a satisfying experience to work with ground gems to make color! All those melting gradations of shades of ultramarine were achieved by many washings in a lye solution. The lye was then dried into crystals that ranged in color from a violent violet to a too-weak blue. These extremes in shade were discarded, and the rest became the source of the medieval artist's ultramarine blue.

Azurite, another heavenly medieval blue, has a silver quality to it. In fact, this rather rare mineral color is often found close to silver veins. Azure crystals were not ground as finely as those used for some of the other mineral-based colors. Azure crystals literally radiated light as they reflected and transmitted the sun's rays through their crushed refracted surfaces. Azurite made a heavenly light-filled blue green that was a beautiful color for rendering draperies. There were ways to make imitation azurite, but as in comparing rhinestones to diamonds, the effect never even approached the original. Imitation azure blue was made from indigo mixed with white lead or lime white and small amounts of water. This imitation azure was thicker, denser, and not as infused with light as the real thing, for lead and indigo are not, after all, rare gleaming gems.

Another alchemized color was copper blue. It was made by hanging plates made of copper over hot vinegar in sealed pots until a green crust formed. This green pigment was then synthesized with lime to produce the shocking bright blue of medieval paintings. Copper blue is a clear, sunlit blue that contains the warmer tones that are missing from ultramarine. Copper blue has the blue of the Mediterranean in it and is the blue of medieval miniatures.

Yellow ochre is another of the natural medieval colors, the color of a seam of sulfur in the earth. Cennini relates the story of how he found a seam of yellow ochre in the side of a hill and excitedly picked out the wrinkle of color with his pen-knife. "For hair and for costumes, I never found a better color than this," he wrote. Ochre was an all-around color, often used in frescoes, and was not so difficult to work up as the gem colors.

Brilliant yellow was made with a poison substance called orpiment. "Beware of touching your mouth with it lest you suffer personal injury," Cennini warned. Mixed with Indian indigo, orpiment made a wonderful grass green. Then there was realgar yellow, and saffron, made, according to Cennini, by mixing the plant with lye. "For the most perfect grass color imaginable" Cennini recommended a little verdigris and three parts saffron. Arzica was a Florentine yellow, a thin color good for illuminations.

Robust medieval orange was made from the poisonous red oxide of lead known as minium. Many pigments were made from deadly poisons, especially those in the white, yellow, and orange color range. Pounding the lead into tiny dust particles must have been dangerous business. Medieval orange was not the same as the metal orange one thinks of today, the one commonly seen as the undercoating of a metal fence to keep the rust from seeping through to the surface. Medieval orange was a more intensely flaming orange. It was the closest color to bright red that was affordable for daily use. They called the shade *color flammeus,* or flame red. It is close to the fire orange found in today's popular Thai silk.

Orange and red were much confused in the Middle Ages. Minium was often confused with vermilion, which was a quite different color. Yet people had trouble distinguishing between them, like Homer with his blues. To increase the confusion, if you closely examine an oil painting, you will often find the two colors, vermilion red and minium orange, used side by side. As in a fire, red and orange commingle but do not quite mix.

Another new medieval mineral color was malachite green, made from the stone. It was a glistening blue and yellow shade, much more dense and intense than forest green. Another green was terre verte, a natural earth color. A green also was made from azurite to which was added the juice of crushed wild plums. Other medieval greens were verdigris green, prepared by exposing copper to vinegar, and sage green, made by mixing terre verte with white lead.

White lead and lime white were the lighteners on the medieval color palette. Little cakes of slaked lime were allowed to dry on rooftops in the sun "to get all the fatness out of them." It was impossible to lighten fresco colors without lime white. The white in the marvelous medieval frescoes of Florence is never the dead American white, but a live white, full of light and color. Even more brilliant was the white made from white lead, another lethal poison that artists worked with.

The black of the Old World color wheel is different from the flat black of America or the lacquered black of the East. Have you ever marveled at how soft-looking soot is? The same velvety quality is found in the black of the early European artist. Carbon black was achieved by burning vine twigs or almond shells. The very finest carbon black was made by burning linseed oil and collecting the soot.

To see all these colors in their full brilliancy, all you need do is look at medieval art, whether it be in the form of enamel, stained glass, paintings, or frescoes. You will notice that there is little brown in these brilliantly colored pictures. Brown was not used much in medieval art. The reason that there is so little brown is the aim of the painter was to produce definite colors, and brown does not have the necessary clarity. Color was a highly developed art, and for people interested in being uplifted to heaven the color of the earth had little appeal.

Metals that accompanied these extravagant colors were of the best, of course. Could anything less than gold or silver enhance lapis lazuli? However silver tarnishes, while gold gleams and sparkles. Often the source of the medieval artists' gold was melted coins, although the practice was forbidden. Gold was also used in powdered form, and gold leaf was another favorite way to apply the precious metal. It would be beaten to the thickness of foil or even the thinnest tissue paper.

You won't find paints made from crushed semiprecious stones at the paint store these days. However, it's always interesting to know what the best product is, and in paint, the medieval period has never been surpassed! In order to really understand the quality of colors made of powdered gems, go to a museum and view a collection of minerals or to a store that sells them. The colors of malachite, lapis lazuli, and azurite are of an intensity to make one gasp. These colors are luminous and often shocking in their brilliance, as if they glowed in the dark as well as in the daylight. They can seem as unexpected and thrilling as a vein of gold in a mound of dirt.

Today there are around thirty commonly used colors. Half that many were available to the artists of the Renaissance. Painters used tricks with color contrast to make up for the color shading they didn't possess. Leonardo was one of the painters who was handicapped by the technology of his times. He could not bear to have his painting delayed by the tedious process of mixing colors and often did not do an adequate job of preparing his canvases. Today some of his precious paintings are in advanced states of disrepair because of his impatience, their surfaces crumbling, the colors not always stabilized. If Leonardo were painting today, he would probably like the speed of acrylic and the oil pastels.

Before the nineteenth century color was what color had always been since ancient times. Even today, however, you will not find the new chemical colors in Old World homes. Whether you go to England, France, or Italy, you will see a much more traditional approach to color than in America, where colors actually have trends. This idea is foreign to Europeans, who approach color in terms of its aging properties. Will the color, for example, be better or worse after a succession of cleanings? Rarely will you find a home on the Continent painted in the latest trendy color. Europeans prefer to do things the way they always have been done, in the tradition of their ancestors. Besides, the colors of their ancestors' belongings are all around them in precious paintings, frescoes, panelings, and objets d'art.

In such cases, one does not decide to throw out the old and start all over, which is often the custom in America. Any new addition to a European home in the way of color must agree with what is already there. Is the popular color called celadon really new? Actually, it's perhaps a few tones lighter than the medieval Italian sage green. If a European wants a color change (and many Americans are Europeans in their home decorating if not in their home address), it must blend with the tapestry, the portraits, the frescoed ceilings, and the heirloom china. Such rooms would rarely be enhanced by the introduction of, say, a fun zebra-striped wall or a grayed-out postmodern color scheme.

English Colors

When I use the term *Continental* I include England. Even though Great Britain is an island and not part of the European continent, when it comes to home decorating its color choices are very much a part of the Continental tradition. The English color wheel revolves around the following ten colors: monarch red, royal purple, sweet pea lavender, leather brown, jonquil yellow, apple green, primrose pink, soft aqua blue (which the English use a lot with creamy beige) deep rose, and racing green. The last, I confess, is one of my top color preferences, and one that is also closely associated with the Rolls-Royce. It is very popular in England to have the outside of a car painted dark green with the interior done in a fawn beige or a bright monarch red.

I have in mind a library for a proper Englishman in those Rolls-Royce colors. The bookshelves are of a dark wood, such as a rich mahogany or walnut. Light colors or bleached-out woods never appear in such a room. On the floor is a rich royal red carpet. At the windows is English racing-green velvet drapery. The jewelry of the room is bright brass.

The upholstery on the sofa is dark green leather framed with brass nailheads. On top of the red carpet there is a small Oriental rug in burgundy, beige, rust, and pale blue. On top of this rug is a mahogany English butler's tray that lifts off the frame. On this tray is a silver tray and on the silver tray there is a decanter and glasses of Galway Irish crystal. A wing chair pulled up to the sofa is upholstered in a deep cordovan leather. For accents and added comfort, there are some old fringed tapestry pillows in dark browns, greens, and reds on the sofa. Hanging from the center of the ceiling is a big brass chandelier with dark green shades around the fixtures. Flanking the fireplace are a pair of chairs slipcovered in a foggy off-green fabric, deeper than celadon, approaching pea-soup green. The slipcovers are piped in brown.

If you were going to do an English drawing room, you would want to use another combination of colors, still in the English mode. You might paint the walls a pale aqua blue with cream-colored trim. On the floor would be a beige rug. The drapes might be in a light aqua blue and beige stripe, and they could be lined with an English chintz in a pattern of big roses on an aqua-blue background. The pelmets (the English word for valances) might have welted diamond-shaped decorations and at each end might be hung a rope tassel in beige and blue. The English drawing room usually contains a number of over-sized upholstered sofas and pull-up chairs. One sofa might be covered in the same chintz used to line the drapery. A pair of chairs might be covered in a velvet with long fringes around the skirt. Accessories could include large bowls filled with blooming roses. The light fixture could be crystal or silver with ornamental light bulbs not covered by shades.

In the English color scheme there is a clarity about the wall color. The English generally tend to put fabrics in practical colors on their chairs and sofas and tend to use more slipcovers than other cultures do. This might be because people spend more time indoors in the English climate than in the climates farther to the south. Another reason the English prefer their colors dark and practical is that in olden times central heating did not exist and fabrics became soot-covered from being exposed to fireplace heating. The cold and wet climate determined colors to a certain degree, although now those darker colors are chosen more for the sake of tradition than for practical reasons. If you want an English look, you must adhere to the tradition of a practical background color or your lighter choice might look a little out of place.

French Colors

When it comes to French colors, there is a different feeling from the English style. French furniture is more ornate and more delicate than English furniture. When I pick French colors, I go for delicate shades to match the furnishings: a very soft banana cream, a muted aqua blue, a delicate salmon that is almost a cantelope, a green that is paler than celadon, a gold gilt, a soft pineapple yellow, and a fawn beige. I don't think a French interior can be done without some feeling of the Far East introduced because the French were known for using Oriental porcelains. Their colors make excellent accessory choices, blending well with the delicate, fragile, and rather pale French colors. I include soft French blue because it works very nicely with the blue-and-white porcelains of the China trade. I would also include what I call Ritz pink, a soft petal pink used in the Ritz Hotel. The tenth color would be that rich beautiful Christian Dior gray, the color of his white-trimmed Avenue Montaigne store in Paris.

In planning a French bedroom color scheme, I would paint the walls a soft yellow, perhaps with a marbleized feeling. If the room was paneled I would use real gold leaf around the frames. The other trim in the room could be a soft banana color. The carpet could contain Aubusson colors of pale green and feature a formalized fan-shaped oval in the center or a cartouche. Other colors in the rug could be soft yellow, beige, gold, and a simple touch of green. The drapery in the room could be a pale green damask lined in a soft yellow to match the walls. The lining might have a watered finish and a design of pink flowers with a green bow. The draperies could be trimmed in a soft yellow and beige and tied back and hung under matching swags and jabots. On the bed I would use the finest linen I could afford, such as white sheets appliquéd in tiny French rosebuds. The French headboard should be canopied. The fabric should be the same as the one used to line the drapes, but here the lining should be a soft green like the carpet. You could also use a great-looking yellow-and-gold cut velvet for a Louis XIV bergère with pillows of light green and pink.

All the other furniture could be painted white and trimmed in gold leaf. There could be a bronze doré chandelier and at the foot of the bed there might be a poudreuse, a makeup table for the lady of the house. On the night tables could be a pair of bronze doré lamps with silk shades. Upholsteries could be in a multitude of different kinds of delicate French silk. At the windows could be white Austrian shades, elaborately fringed and trimmed. As for the ceiling, you could paint it light blue like the sky and give it white and pink painted clouds with an angel in each corner. That treatment would be authentically traditional. The French like to bring the heavens inside.

Italian Colors

The Italian color wheel is as different from the French as the French color wheel is different from the English. The Italian colors are Venetian blue, a watery aqua blue; silver gray, which is a deeper gray than the French gray; Tuscan clay, that bright Italian terra-cotta; Carrara black; and Renaissance red, a sumptuous color without which an Italian room would not be Italian. There is also a fresco green the shade of grape leaves, the deep green of a leaf that spends its time in the full hot sun, not a forest green like the robust English greens or the delicate celadon green of the French palette. There must be a gold to accompany the Renaissance red, as well as an eggplant, a washed-out marble pink, and a salmon-colored terra rosa.

If I were to design a dining room in Italian colors, the table might be glass-topped and have a wood pedestal base of silver and gold leaf. A Venetian light fixture in light aqua, pink, and white glass with twelve or fourteen candelabra might hang above the table. The Italians like their hanging fixtures large scale. Around the table might be Italian-style chairs painted salmon and trimmed in silver. The panels might be covered in a Fortuny watered silk made by the Fortuny factories in Venice. The reverse side of the fabric might be silver gray and the right side a silvery salmon. The entire room could be outlined with silver trim, and the areas between the silver trim painted salmon. The upholstery fabric could be Fortuny in a salmon silk except for the backs of the chairs, where you could use the reverse side of the Fortuny fabric used in the panels.

An enormous buffet could be painted silver and trimmed in a light apple shade of green. Above this buffet might be placed an enormous Venetian mirror and a pair of Venetian candelabra that match the ceiling light fixture in design, with light aqua, light pink, and clear glass leaves and flowers. On the walls could be enormous portraits in heavy frames that are Renaissance in feeling. The floor might be pink Italian marble with a border of black marble. Huge marble pedestals in each corner of the room could hold vases filled with long-stemmed peach-color roses. On the table might be silver goblets and a centerpiece of grapes, oranges, and nectarines. The Italian linen runner and the table mats could be appliquéd and the ceiling overhead frescoed.

Oriental Colors

Oriental colors are jade colors that range from red to white to green and also aqua. They are cooled-out colors with a subtle

Color Magic

100

glow. There is no harsh white in the Orient, but there is ivory and soapstone. Everything has a gleam. China was first known as the "Land of the Silk People" by the Greeks and Romans. Silk takes brilliant dyes and those brilliant, clear, boisterous colors are the colors of the Orient. There are no pastels here, no earth colors, only the rich reds, yellows, purples, greens, and turquoise blues of silk.

The color of silk mellows as it ages, which is one of silk's great advantages. The emperor's summer robe was made from bright yellow silk. On it was lavish embroidery, another Oriental color source. Colors had meanings far different from our own. Red and yellow are not the colors of the sun in the Orient. They represent the phoenix and the hare. The four points of the compass are represented by black, red, blue, and white. Water is green, fire red, and earth not brown but white.

Oriental color is also the color of glazes, especially the pale green of celadonware, which the French long ago appropriated for their own. There is also yellow, russet, black, and blood red. The enamel colors of the Orient are similar to the colors of the Middle Ages and include clear cobalt blue, copper green, iron red, manganese violet, and crimson.

Lacquer was made from the sap of the precious Oriental tree *Rhus vernicifera.* Lacquer colors are turquoise and slate blue, wine red and rose red, white, plum, and dark purple.

Another source of Oriental color is found in the treasured cloisonné enamel colors, a craft learned from the Arabs. Each color is encased in wire so that when the piece is fired the colors do not run together. Cloisonné blue has no lead oxide in it, a marvel to the West. Another gorgeous cloisonné color is Ming pink.

Perhaps the most popular Oriental color sources are rug colors. The dyes used in Oriental rugs are still largely made from vegetable sources. These colors are restrained but rich. The nomad rug of gray and brown in natural wool colors is a neutral look in Oriental rugs. The sources of the rich colors are the indigo plant for blue, madder root for red, saffron for yellow, ripe turmeric berries for green, walnut shells for brown, and brazilwood for black.

My Oriental color wheel is made up of cinnabar, jade green, paprika orange, mother-of-pearl, black lacquer, metallic gold, porcelain blue, Chinese red, turquoise, rose quartz, and saffron. Oriental colors are all strong and clear. Think of Shanghai lacquer red used with black and gold on the beautiful temples and houses. The lacquer colors to me are the most beautiful: the red, black, rust, and cinnabar colors. The Oriental look is the look of lacquer with its cleanliness, simplicity, and sheen.

For a room done in the Oriental manner you might paper the walls in a saffron Thai silk fabric and put down paprika carpets. At the windows, you might use a pink, turquoise, red, and black Chinese figured pattern on an orange-gold background fabric. You might place a big carved opium bed in the middle of the room dressed in a soft kumquat orange offset with russet chairs. Two large jade lamps could sit on black teak chests with Oriental brass hardware placed on either side of the bed. On the opposite side of the room could be an Oriental settee with an all-wood frame, its seat cushion covered in a cinnabar red. Next to it could be a pair of Chinese garden seats. Oriental trunks lacquered in cinnabar red could sit on small stands. The room might have a painted white ceiling with a pagoda-shaped Chinese light fixture made of black lacquer with frosted panels.

In essence, this Oriental room has a spicy feeling to it, from the saffron walls to the paprika carpet. These colors, together with the teak and the jade, give the room a feeling of mystery. At the entrance to the room, I would have a pair of Chinese carved teakwood pedestals with little marble tops on which could sit large Oriental temple jars. Above the sofa I would hang a panel inlaid with mother-of-pearl, ivory, and semiprecious stones like jade and blue quartz.

Americana Colors

America is a continent unto itself, and as in Europe, light and climate determine much about our decorating style. Traditional Americana may not have as many centuries behind it as the much older European styles, but it is as well loved and cherished as the Old World decorative traditions.

In America there are traditional styles that say seaside Maine or Kentucky plantation or Adirondack retreat, but the colors that work best in the widely varying climates and topographies of this vast country of ours are the colors that relate to local nature and local history. Modern colors are exciting in urban and suburban areas, but when nature occupies the better part of the landscape, then its colors become the most important for you to use in selecting your color scheme.

The colors of Americana are the colors that were yielded up in the pre-nineteenth-century backyard dye pot. There is little evidence in the Americana color wheel of malachite blue, royal purple, vermilion, ultramarine, or any of the glistening colors produced by precious and semiprecious minerals or by the coloring juices of tiny forms of animal life. Such extravagance is simply not at home in the Americana style, which relies on colors yielded by the dipping in vegetable dyes of honest cotton, linen, and wool. If you limit your Americana color palette to those colors that could be produced by vegetation growing in your area, you will be making no wrong color choices.

Traditional Americana colors from the backyard vegetable

dye pot make up a rich and wonderful natural color wheel: indigo blue, barn red, wheat, mustard, buttercup yellow, dusky gray, spring green, madder red, tobacco, and summer green. A favorite Americana color is yellow. Could it be because so many things in nature contain pigments that produce yellow? If you like yellow, think of pure glistening yellows and not the dense green yellows of the modern color palette.

Yellow dye comes from nature's local supplies of leaves, fruit, flowers, roots, and bark. Even the skin of an onion yields a bright fall yellow. Pale gold, buttercup, cream, sand, wheat, amber, and rust: these are shades of Americana yellow. If you want to take your local landscape into consideration, there's bound to be one or more likely sources of yellow growing in your neighborhood: goldenrod, Osage orange, lady's-purse, sagebrush, mullein, marigolds, lichen, mushrooms, and milk-wood.

Americana green, of course, is nature green. It's not a city-traffic-light green or a rich, opulent mineral green but the alive green of the trees and grasses of your neighborhood. Country greens for dyes are often made from leaves. A deep green comes from purple coleus leaves. Pine needles yield olive green, snapdragon flowers make a soft spring green, and purple foxglove give close to a chartreuse. Citron green is made from the leaves of heather, aster, and the common privet. The lily-of-the-valley flower makes a pale, clear green. Blue lupine makes midsummer green and seaweed makes silver green. Green is an important Americana color, but it must have life to it. To decide whether a swatch of green you are considering should be used in your Americana decor, lay some leaves and flowers around it and decide whether it blends or sticks out at you like something alien and unnatural. If you choose a natural fabric, you don't have to be a purist about your dyes. Perfectly respectable colors come out of the chemical vat, but those colors are at their best in a natural fabric, because frequent washing will improve the color and texture of the surface.

Blues and purples are also readily available in nature. Red and purple hollyhock petals yield a clear, pale blue that is particularly lovely, as do crushed berries of many kinds. However, the most important Americana blue is an import. Like the ancients of the Old World, America's favorite blue is a shade of indigo. Sky blue is the first blue to be yielded as a fabric is dropped into an indigo pot, swirled around, and brought up on a stick. If sky blue is too light, another dip will yield dusky blue, and eventually you will arrive at that most popular shade of all, jeans blue. Indigo blue from a chemical dye should never yield a loud color. It should be dense and deep, but should not stand out and be too insistent.

Slate blue to gray are other important segments of the Americana color wheel. Gray is a common color in nature, where it accents light and shadows. Even the most delicate gray in nature is infused with light. This is no place for trendy flannel gray. Down-home gray is more in the pewter family, and is often purple-hued like shadows on snow. It has a light to it that the urban gray colors do not. Vegetable fibers that yield gray dyes are sunflower seeds, rhododendron leaves, mulberry fruit, and the green shoots of the blackberry bush.

White in the country-color spectrum is not the dead white of the city. It always has a tinge of yellow or blue in it. Stark white is not an Americana country color and should be toned down to a bone white or even as far as a mushroom white. Country white is arrived at by a bleaching process. Linen, cotton, and wool can all be bleached to the desired color of whiteness without ever looking dead the way urban white can look. Country sheets are often white and are dried on the grass to be bleached by the sun. Americana white has just that sun-bleached quality.

Americana red is rarely the lavish and costly European crimson, scarlet, or vermilion. A touch of this red is possible in colorful accessories, but too much of a brilliant shade of red in wall, fabric, or floor covering isn't appropriate. The frugal

American homemaker who made everything at home, laboriously and by hand, was known for making much out of little.
Rarely was expensive imported vermilion or Aztec red used in
the Americana home. It was too lavish. Red from vegetable
dyes is never as bright and brilliant as the red produced from
minerals, insects, or shellfish, but a gorgeous barn red and
some lovely pinks can be produced using lichen, bloodroot,
beets, and many types of berries. A rich salmon shade comes
from a certain orange mushroom and russula yields up a shell
pink.

Earth colors of the umber family are also important in an
Americana home. Damp, rich earth is an amalgam of browns,
beiges, and near blacks. These colors don't have a sheen, but
they must be full-bodied. Brown is produced by many things
in nature: acorn shells, black walnuts, sumac seeds, and beech
leaves. A good, rich country brown is essential in the
Americana color palette.

In a traditional Americana room you could paint all the
walls green and use a pink, red, and green floral chintz with a
blue-and-white-striped background and pink pillows. You
might add a little Oriental influence like a Coromandel coffee
table in black, because that would be entirely appropriate to
the Americana tradition. You could hang a knotted hooked rug
on the wall and another printed fabric in green tones at the
window.

Colonial Colors

The style of Americana has a traditional period that corresponds to historical European styles: American Colonial. These
are the colors you will see at Williamsburg and Monticello:

slate blue, goldenrod yellow, fawn beige, boxwood green, the muted green of treenware, barn red, pewter gray, indigo blue, indigo violet, and whitewash white.

If you are planning a living room in the Colonial style, you could begin by painting the walls a slate blue and putting around the top of the walls where they meet the ceiling a stencil of fawn beige and whitewash. The floors could be stained a rich tobacco color.

For a sofa you might choose a small tweed or print in a woven fabric that is goldenrod yellow and white. The sofa could have a pine frame in the Empire style. You could pick a wing chair for the room and cover it in a plaid of goldenrod yellow, beige, and blue gray. For floor covering, you could find a good-looking cotton rug of yellows, whites, and beige. For under your coffee table, you could use an old hooked rug with a design of a cat or an arrangement of garden flowers. For lamps you could choose pewter bases with cream-white pierced shades. Pewter is the jewelry of the Colonial home, as is black wrought iron.

For pillows, you might use the barn red color against the goldenrod sofa. For an added touch, you could tint the ceiling with just a hint of goldenrod so that when light from the pierced lampshades was thrown on the ceiling there would be a reflecting glow of color throughout the room. I would also have a terra-cotta-colored brick fireplace wall. On the mantel above the fireplace I would display a group of pewter plates, blue-and-white early Colonial plates, or Rockinghamware in brown and beige. I would use a few pieces of painted furniture like a dry sink lined in zinc or pewter that had a slightly worn blue patina. I would use simple drapery at the windows in this Colonial living room such as natural unbleached cotton curtains. I might add an old basket filled with dried goldenrod flowers and use some good-looking calicos or woven fabrics, or ready-made quilts, as throws for the sofa or wing chair. If you found a seasoned deacon's bench in a natural stain, you could make a pad for it in a simple slate blue.

Regional Americana Styles

There are special colors that define different styles of Americana around the country. When you say Florida and Southern California to me, I see beige, light blue, soft green, pink, violet, and yellow. When I think of Boston, I see burgundy, dark blue, rich green, and beige. When I think of Virginia, I have in mind a softer green, a bluer gray, a Williamsburg green, peach, and riding-breeches tan. When I think of Santa Fe, New Mexico, I see rust, terra-cotta, beige, cactus green, sand-dune white, sunlight blue, and orange—dry colors primarily in tones of sand, rust, and orange.

For Oregon and the Pacific Northwest I see dark forest greens, a strong brown, a clean blue, a salmon and a lobster orange, winter white, and accent colors of orangey red and Rocky Mountain purple. When I see Chicago I see gray walls and postmodern colors of blue gray and dusty rose. All the areas of the country are different to me in terms of color, and I have to keep each locality's colors in mind whenever I plan an indoor color scheme.

When I think of New Orleans, I see yellow walls with chandeliers and a strong French influence; dining-room chairs, for example, painted in the soft French blue and soft multicolored Aubusson rugs. When I think of Maine, I see brown wicker and gray-painted floors and chintzes with dark backgrounds. Pine green, strong yellow, and a combination of blues —Delft, navy, and soft blue—are all right for Maine. I can imagine a whole room in Maine done in an array of greens, from celadon to dark pine with a print that uses a beige background. A sofa could be covered in burgundy, green, and brown with accents of light blue.

Southampton, Long Island, to me is white chintzes and ruffles and linens with a welted trim, often in a contrasting color. I see painted floors in green with white painted flowers and wicker furniture. I like to include a soft yellow in a French provincial Southampton room or in a Palm Beach environment. The softer colors are more suitable to the Florida setting. The color of Florida does not look the same as the color of Long Island and the difference is in the light. Any color I consider is looked at in the light of where it is going, whether it's for a bedroom in the Northeast or a desert dining room in the Southwest. Light is the most important and the most variable of all the ingredients that go into color magic.

California to me is a pattern place, where people tend to use strong colors. I've seen paisley designs in purple and red and royal blue that worked successfully in California. For California, I see a lot of brown and orange paisleys or an orange flower on a beige background with big green leaves. California is big scale all the way—big proportions in lamps, overscaled French provincial furniture. Painted chair frames are very California to me. Burgundy is a popular color for frames, for instance, used with a blue trim and with seats covered in a crisscross pattern of burgundy and blue on beige. Californians often use a lot of color on one piece, such as two different upholstery fabrics on one chair. The back might be solid burgundy, the seat blue welted in blue and red. I think Californians like to overstate because it fills up space. There's a sense of formality in the overscale that's unique to California. The formal California colors are wine, royal blue, rich purple, and gold. These are often picked as backgrounds in prints. Against these colors, Californians like to mix florals and geometrics.

Island-Living Colors

There is a special color spectrum for island living. In that spectrum I include the Virgin Islands, Hawaii, Puerto Rico, Florida, and Southern California as well as the southern regions bordering the Gulf of Mexico where one finds real tropical living. The spectrum for island living is straw, aqua blue, coral, sun yellow, hibiscus red, jungle green, lime green, abalone pink, white, and papaya orange. These colors spell tropical island to me.

Here is a sun-room for a tropical island. These indoor/outdoor rooms are often off the kitchen and usually screened. I would paint the ceiling in sun-yellow-and-white stripes, as if it were an awning. I would use jungle green and citrus green in a frond pattern in the curtains. The furniture could be natural wheat rattan covered in papaya orange and accented with pillows of jungle green and lime green. In front of the sofa might be a rattan coffee table. The pull-up chairs could be covered in lemon yellow. Outside would be an aqua-blue pool.

This color scheme can work with both shades of green—lime and jungle—and any of the other colors in the tropical spectrum. You could also use a papaya and white stripe or an aqua and white stripe. Shell-pink coral or straw could be alternated with white stripes, as well. The exception would be hibiscus red, which should be used only as a floral accent, so powerful a color is it. This red is best used only in the form of the flower itself. There's so much of this lush color around naturally in the tropics, where trees burst into bloom in flaming orange.

I like walls painted white in the islands. There's something wonderful about the purity of light when the sun hits white stucco walls. The reflection of that light with the aqua-blue sea is color enough. But island decorating is not applicable to points north. Like wearing summer white too early or too late, it is inappropriate to use these colors in northern light. The island palette may be more limited than some of the other color spectrums, but these colors are remarkably easy to work with, because you have the sun on your side.

There's a special color combination unique to the island of Bermuda: pink and white. Many of the houses are painted in these colors and even the coral sand is pink and white. The light is so strong that fabric colors should be unidentifiable and soft. There should be no strong contrast among the colors. A light green background might have a water lily flower on it in a white and beige or a soft pink, but all the colors should have the same value—a soft, soothing, cooling quality, as if they had been bleached by many summers in the sun.

Victorian Americana Colors

Another popular traditional Americana style is Victorian. In terms of color, it poses many problems. Halfway through the Victorian era, in 1856, the world of color changed completely. Alcohol was added to coal tar and a new color of violet was born from what became known as aniline dye. The French named this new color *mauve* after the purple of the mallow flower. For those unfamiliar with that flower, it is the dusty blued-down lavender of Victorian times.

The aniline dye spectrum was expanded to include black, malachite green, and burnt red. These aniline colors all fade, some drastically. Black fades to a dark moss green, burnt red to sepia. It's funny how in fashion today's discovery becomes tomorrow's old look and then eventually the future's revival.

The colors of the aniline dye pot that were all the rage in the age of Victoria are back. These gray-washed, toned-down mauve-to-bluish-red colors have become popular again. Today they are known as the postmodern colors, about which more later. Victoria reigns again from the living room to the boardroom to the airport waiting room.

My approach to Victorian colors is different: Let the sun shine in. The reason I like light-struck Victorian colors is that everything else about the look is so heavy. The period was very regal in its pretenses with a lot of red-on-red, burgundy-on-gray, and rose-on-rose in flocked wallpaper. Other favorite Victorian colors are deep gray and blue green, often used in velvet to cover sofas. With such a sofa covering today you might use big muted roses with blue-green leaves. Your walls could be the same blue green with white trim.

Rose-colored velvet drapes could be used at the window, but not a dusty rose. You could choose instead a luscious rose that might appear in a Victorian garden. Victorian velvet draperies look good lavishly hung from ornate brass poles that match a large brass light fixture suspended from the ceiling. Another upholstery choice would be chintz in the faded colors of blue-green roses on brown. In a true Victorian room there is a sense that the flowers had lost their color and died by the time the artist began to paint them for a fabric design.

There's a brown-red cast to authentic Victorian colors and a tintype feeling in most of the tones—from gray to rose to green—that is spiritless to me, as spiritless as I find the colors of the postmodern revival. Raw aniline dye was far from perfect. When it faded, it did not always fade attractively. Victorians, eager for color they could afford, took their chances and lived with their tintype colors.

The Victorians did not make contrasting color statements. For instance, if they had brown woodwork, they picked a color for the walls that did not contrast with the woodwork. The wall and the woodwork would be in the same gradation of color. In the traditional Victorian room there would also be a lot of buttoned and tufted effects, even on the walls. Victorians would even tuft and button the backs of doors. These wall treatments would often be done not in the clear English hunter green but the puce-tinged office green the English are rather fond of to this day.

From Victorian to Postmodern

Victoria's influence extended well into the twentieth century. However, in the early part of this century another influence from the East arrived in Europe, whence so much of American taste in decor was imported. That Eastern influence was the Ballet Russe, which was the rage of Paris before World War I. Onstage and offstage, these exotic Russian dancers wore costumes in brilliant, luminous, and exotic colors like bright magenta, orange, and lustrous aquamarine.

In a color sense the 1920s weren't all that roaring. In fact, the color choices of the period were rather subdued. Gray, navy and white, beige and a cool Nordic blue were favorites, as well as brown. In this Gatsby era of the blazer and summer whites, the background lacked color as if to show off the colorful antics of the people of the times to better effect.

The Depression colors of the 1930s are those that foster feelings of security: dark wine, chocolate, and bottle green. These colors could be washed again and again, and there was nothing frivolous about them. The luxury of experimenting with color was not within the means of most people during the Depression. They lived with their dark, drab, but secure colors at home and dreamed in black and white of satin and chiffon at the movies. World War II certainly did nothing to spruce up the scene. Military colors returned again, raw materials and quality goods went into the war effort, and neutral colors continued to be the norm.

In the 1940s, furniture was much more blond than it had been for generations. This was also the beginning of the era of plastic in hardware. Much of the furniture was rather square and dreary. It was the period of chartreuse harlequin lamps accompanied by a black porcelain cat, and a time when accessories were much darker than the furniture. Frank Lloyd Wright decided to design fabrics, and each one was uglier than the next, with interplays of geometric shapes, as if someone had sat down with a T-square to design them. The designs were printed on fiberglass, one of the new fabrics in the beginning of the synthetic era. Wright's designs remind me of a game my children had when they were babies, where they had to put the round peg in the round hole, and the square peg in the square hole. The colors of these fabrics have no more to recommend them to me than do the designs. I believe they must have been influenced by the success of Howard Johnson, for there are many in turquoise and orange with a touch of brown. You have to take this look with a lot of whimsy, if at all.

Other popular decorating touches of the time included the enormous round plastic hassock in turquoise or turquoise and white in alternating sections. It was also the era of the kitchen chair in red or brown plastic vinyl and shiny steel. Having been considered junk for many years, they are now coming back into vogue and occasionally can be picked up at yard sales. The chairs were sturdy and many have survived.

In a recent off-Broadway musical *Pump Boys and Dinettes,* set in a diner next door to a filling station, the chorus boys pumped gas and the chorus girls were the diner waitresses. The counter for this set was red plastic with silver edging. The tableware was the authentic melamine down to the orange and aqua ashtrays in futuristic designs. It's too bad the color turquoise has been reduced to those pathetic plastic representations. When I think of the beginnings of plastic, I think of two colors: orange and turquoise, both in shades never before seen on earth. I think the shock of these shades has stuck with entire generations of home decorators, who shun them to this day.

With the advent of the 1950s and postwar prosperity, as all those new baby-boom families moved into their own homes, there was a sudden surge of interest in home decorating across the land. Modern newlyweds fell for the pastel rage. After the absence of light color for so many years, people found that pastels were just what they wanted in their new homes. Furniture was light-colored in its wood as well. The age of blond Hollywood modern had been born at the movies.

In the 1960s came another color revolution. Suddenly there was an explosion of color. Old guidelines for the use of color became obsolete overnight, and there was a release of color energy that virtually throbbed on the walls. The baby-boom generation was finally old enough to have its own pads and many of them were influenced by the popularity of psychedelic colors. Neon was also very big.

By the 1970s most people had fallen out of love with their psychedelic decor. They were interested in a look that was a lot less strident and a lot more natural. The 1970s was the era of environmentalism and every home became crowded with plants. There were plants in the windows, plants hanging from the ceiling, and plants sitting next to you on the floor. After a while people began to realize that a jungle of plants didn't make a decorating statement. It *became* the decorating statement. Plants are still used a great deal these days, but not en masse as they were in this period.

Something else happened in the 1970s that affected home decor very much. Trade was reestablished with mainland China and people began learning about quality Oriental imports. In the past "Made in Taiwan" was a way of saying cheap and tacky. But "Made in Peking" has since the time of Marco

Polo been a way of describing quality goods. The ancient arts of China are flooding the market today and are still being made in the time-honored way. If you wish, you can buy an Oriental table of teak inlaid with mother-of-pearl and semiprecious gems, and then lacquered with a substance made of resin, the precious Oriental lac, and cashews. The creation of each piece is a six-year process that has not changed since ancient times. Since the 1970s, when the American public first was exposed to vast amounts of quality Oriental goods, the interest in the Far East has greatly increased.

The 1970s also saw the mass-marketing of quality goods in this country in places like Conran's. Until the economy began to stagger under the oil crisis, it was a time of prosperity for a lot of people who were just developing good taste in home furnishings, food, and wines.

The current age is one of decorative refinement, but also an age of conformity. It is a period heavily influenced by cool colors, tranquil curves, and high-gloss Oriental lacquer surfaces. The look is called *postmodern,* and I think it displays, as trends always do, where we all are. In fact, we're living in a toned-down time. It's Chinese minus the brilliant color. It's Art Deco without the glitz. It's a time when emotions are quieted and there is a great desire for a return to the tranquil in one's life as well as in one's home environment.

"Too cool to love" could be the slogan of today. That's the way the postmodern room impresses me: stylish, but lacking warmth. Dorothy Draper used to say of the 1930s that the modern style was black, white, and empty. Postmodern isn't black, white, and empty but beige, gray, black, white, and empty. At least today times are slightly less bleak in terms of color.

The main feature of postmodern color to me is that it isn't real. Postmodern color is grayed out, beiged out, or whited out, but not blacked out. There are no extremes of color just as there are no extremes of anything in the postmodern style.

It's interesting to me, while driving down the highways of America, to see what colors people choose in their cars. Today the colors are as man-made as the cars, pure chemical colors. There's a gray, a brown red, a green puce, and a gray taupe. As colors they are nothingburgers. Like the fashion in dress, car-color choice in the 1980s is toned down and on the blue-gray side. There's not a bit of bright red to be seen.

The middle class today is more achievement-oriented than ever because of the economic situation. Its members always dress more somberly than the lower economic classes, for whom achievement is much less of a possibility. But today's middle class is conservative. Indeed, as conservative in its dress as people were in the era of the gray-flannel suit. The toned-down and subdued color trend of the eighties means to me that people are into playing it safe. This is not a time for big splashy drama and a whole lot of individuality. People don't want to take many decorating risks or come up with anything shocking in their manner of dress.

The postmodern colors are a sandy, frosted gray beige called greige, a mauve-hued heather, a claret, flannel gray, dusty rose, watered aquamarine, and amber orange, a color more watered down than peach. These postmodern colors are hard to describe. Yellow is not among them. It's too bright. Neither is there a real blue. It's too primary. No statement louder than claret is made in the postmodern color range, which is completed by a dusty raspberry, slate black, and dead white.

These postmodern colors are to me no-colors, neither fish nor fowl, neither one thing nor another. If you take a flower pattern, photograph it in black and white, and then superimpose gradations of rose and beige on it, that's postmodern color. Nearly every upscale restaurant and gift shop around the country now has postmodern decor. The surfaces are all ultra high gloss. The pottery gleams and the lacquer shines. It's a surface look and that surface is slick. There are no hard edges in the postmodern look and I mean that literally. The furniture is designed with deeply rounded corners. Credenzas often are bolted to a wall, eliminating the need for legs. The harsh lines of the chrome chair have been replaced by rounded curves on glossy painted furniture in those postmodern colors. Nearly all the wood in the postmodern style is painted and then given a high lacquer finish. What few natural woods there are in the mahogany and Far Eastern cypress range are richly burled and very expensive.

It used to be that schools were painted in Mondrian colors: big squares of primary colors. For the past few years, new schools have been given the postmodern color treatment. Instead of the happy Crayola primaries in which schools were painted the last time you may have looked, they are now being painted in dark grape and bright acid green, fantasy colors brighter than in the adult postmodern spectrum, but still nothing anyone could readily identify. It's as if someone had poured some gray or brown into each of the primary paint cans and then painted the walls.

If you look at the dress of the successful businessman of today, you will notice he reflects the cooled-down, postmodern style as well. He will wear only two or three shades at one time. The only color he brings in is introduced in a very modest way in his tie. If you use nontraditional colors or patterns in the business world of today, you run the risk of giving out the message that you are different and have no intention of fitting in. There are no love beads around anymore among the corporate set. These days, the only way the successful executive lets loose in his dress is by arriving at the office in his jogging shoes, with his business shoes in a knapsack on his back.

If you sit in the lobby of any major hotel in New York, Chicago, Dallas, or San Francisco, the most likely color you will see is gray. We have indeed returned to a gray-flannel era in men's suits. A man who wears a black suit had better have the authority to back it up. A man with no aura of power who wears a black suit runs the risk of appearing ridiculous.

The upholstered pieces of the postmodern era are nearly soft sculptures, often armless and rather bulbous. There is no tuck-in seat or tufted back. Oftentimes, the look is more like a banquette than a sofa. Bedroom furniture features the floating bed, a lacquered frame with two winglike attachments that serve as legless nightstands. The jewelry for the postmodern look is frosted, hammered, and never shiny. Glass is frosted and tinted with mottled surfaces. Nothing is clear. There is no longer a trace of Lucite and chrome.

Lamps are round as is nearly everything, whether mirrors, chairs, or chests of drawers. There is a fondness for the curvilinear line of Art Deco. A lot of money was lavished in the 1930s on a gorgeous skyscraper look that, as in the period of the Gothic cathedral, sent the eyes heavenward, although not to marvel at the Almighty but at the mighty works of man. I think the Art Deco revival was a long time in coming. The furniture and appointments are well designed and of high quality. Keep your eye out for Art Deco when you go around to antiques stores or yard sales. You might be surprised to discover that you really like it. For one thing, it will remind you of wonderful old movies with the likes of Greta Garbo, Ginger Rogers, and Fred Astaire.

The postmodern look breaks away from the square and the cube, the right-angled line and the harsh definition. Even the lines between colors are broken down. Colors are not clearly this or that. It is as though the shock of all those contrasts of the past was too much. People seem to have decided there has been too much excitement in their lives and that it's time to lower the decibels all around, including in color and line. Many people find the postmodern look very restful. They really take to the new statement it makes and find themselves wanting it first in a bedroom and then in a dining room and soon all over the house. They say moving among its rooms makes them feel relaxed.

For a room in the postmodern style, I might start with a gray-rose wall and a sofa in gray. The carpet could be gray rose as well. Above the softly curved sofa could be a round mirror with a lacquered frame in gray rose. There also might be a pair of curved end tables lacquered gray rose, and on those end tables might be two Art Deco ceramic lamps. The large lamp-shades might be painted gray outside and white inside. A glass-topped coffee table could be frosted glass, lit from below, with a frosted glass sculpture on it.

Perhaps you are attracted to the way the postmodern design works as a neutral background for quality collectibles. For a room that is basically beige in the postmodern style, I would have beige walls and a round beige coffee table with a high-gloss lacquer and a sleek black glass top. The modern look of the room would come from the use of the architectural beige and white against the beige modern-textured carpet, perhaps a natural wool Berber. A modern painting would bring in color as would an ornate lacquered chair. Vertical blinds would take away all fullness to the windows. A marble-top table could hold an agate-colored vase filled with spotted calla lilies. This room would attractively display many a fine piece of art. However, the art must be of high quality or the look will not be authentically postmodern.

American Modern

American modern is a style that features the hot paint-box primary colors: royal blue, white, bright red, yellow, bright green, turquoise, black, magenta, orange, and raspberry. The modern rooms from the 1950s to the 1970s were rooms that had a strong feeling of color about them.

For example, let's take a modern New York apartment building where you might choose to decorate a room in the 1950s style. This was the beginning of the geometric era, so you could put down a geometric wall-to-wall carpet in brown, white, and cocoa. The scale of the design should be big. The walls could be painted in a bright primary yellow lacquer. The sectional sofa in front of that wall could be brown and on the sofa could be bright yellow and red pillows. If the height of the ceiling is sufficient, it, too, could be painted a rich chocolate brown.

The lamps could be white ginger jars with big white accordion-pleated shades with brown cords. Over the sofa could hang a large modern painting that had yellow and red predominating, with a touch of green. The coffee table should be expansive and glass-topped. There could be two Barcelona chairs, the familiar stainless steel chairs once seen in every bank lobby, covered in brown leather. The window could be treated not with drapery or shutters but with the vertical blind, which was a big fifties statement and continues to be so, even for the postmodernists. This room will say classic American modern.

The American modern bedroom could have a window treatment of white shades. In such a room, the bed could be set up on a pedestal carpeted in solid brown. The bedside tables could be white laminate with no hardware on them. Instead, the drawers would have push panels. The light for the headboard could be set in above the bed. Over the bed might be a panel painted red. On the headboard could be a modern Giacometti-like sculpture. In the corner of the room might stand a plastic waterfall, circa 1960, featuring a series of water bowls with a light and motor, the water dripping from one level to the next.

On the pedestal bed might be a tight-fitting bedspread the color of the carpet, or perhaps designed with a big chevron print so popular during the period. There could be other sixties favorites in the room, an arc light in chrome and some sling pull-up chairs in red or brown. The look of this room became dated very quickly, but it now says "sixties modern" to many people the way a plain pine board chest says Early American.

Making Color Magic

When I begin working with clients on color for their entire home, I have to be very sure where their color preferences lie, because there has to be a coordination of color from the front door to the back and all through the house. The coordination of color begins at the beginning: in the entryway. From there it proceeds into the living room and on into all the other rooms, upstairs and down.

But how do you begin? By connecting and coordinating—with color. You do this the same way you dress in the morning. When most people combine colors in an outfit, they wear three. When creating a wardrobe of color for your house, you start in much the same way, with three colors. Then you add touches of new colors, while dropping others, as you move from room to room.

The colors should create a feeling of harmony. If the colors in a well-designed house were music, they would be a symphony.

I always think it's fascinating to examine the way artists apply colors in a painting, one by one. But because you have to be able to conceptualize color harmony to foresee the end result at the beginning of the process, I never like people to see rooms in the early stages of decoration. Most people can't get the full color picture, because they don't understand color magic. They begin to analyze each color as it is put on separately. When an artist begins a canvas, he or she may begin with white and some of the lighter tones. Next time he or she may apply black and brown, and you may get an entirely new feeling about the painting. But if on top of that the artist starts adding pinks and yellows, the painting changes once again. In the same way, you can't analyze color in a room until the decorating process is complete. Much can change during the final stages when even more colors are added in lamps, pillow accents, carpets, and draperies. You can't walk into a dark green room with beige trim and have any idea what the end result will be unless you know how to apply color magic the way artists and experts in home decorating do.

Although the concept of *color coordination* isn't all that difficult, there are many bad examples to avoid following. Neither the department store "suite" of furnishings nor the model home or apartment with each room done in a different style is the way to go. Over the years there has been an emphasis on the single-room concept of decorating. The White House does have a Blue Room and a Red Room, but there the different rooms happen to work together because they are based on the concept of *color connectives.*

Let us begin with a conservative house in basically neutral colors and coordinate it from front to back. We might start with a wallpaper in the hall that is predominantly ecru beige. All through the house, the trim would be painted in this creamy ecru beige, one of the "safe" colors. "Paint it eggshell" is one of the things people say when they're uncertain what to do. But I've seen white, brown, and even blue eggs! Nevertheless, of all the colors eggs come in, I would choose the nondescript taupey off-white that most people call beige as one of our three conservative colors. Then we could paint the ceilings throughout the house a ceiling or "dead" white, one that has no preponderance of any color.

For the hall then, where the color-coordinating begins, we could choose a wallpaper with a soft geometric design in eggshell, white, and a dash of pumpkin. There also could be a stripe of green running through it. Or, you could choose a floral design in green, beige, and pumpkin. When we get to the living-room walls, we could feature a color from the wallpaper—pumpkin. Then we could put down a beige carpet and take the leaf green from the wallpaper in the hallway and use it on the sofa. It could be velvet, a woven leaf-green tweed, or even a plaid of green, beige, and white in a country house.

On the two pull-up chairs (perhaps wing chairs if the setting is traditional) you could use a fabric that also matches the green in the wallpaper in the hall. If you couldn't find a solid green that pleases you, you could look for a stripe. I have always believed that the stripe is the best and easiest decorating device. This stripe could be in a beige, white, and rust, the latter another new addition to the compatible color symphony. Above the sofa, you could hang a wonderful autumnal scenic painting. In that painting might be autumn hills with rust-colored leaves, cold blue water, clear blue sky, and late-in-the-year green. With this painting almost all the colors would have been introduced with which you could decorate your home. As for living-room drapery, we could put up a beige linen against those gleaming pumpkin walls and trim the drapery in a pumpkin, white, and goldenrod yellow braid. In a very subtle way we would now be introducing yet another color—yellow. You might also use yellow in living-room pillow accents in a goldenrod shade. Sunburst-yellow lamps could be placed on end tables.

Yellow prepares the way for the major color in the next room. It is the color connective. Yellow accents in the living room introduce the color that you could paint your dining-room walls. Your eye moves from pumpkin to appetite-stimulating goldenrod without feeling any shock waves. In the dining room you could use the green of your living-room sofa on the dining-room chair seats. Yellow drapery could have undercurtains of an ecru color, the same color as in the entry-hall wallpaper.

The same color coordination could be carried out from room to room. For instance, you could paint the master bedroom soft, light October blue, the color of the sky in the painting in the living room. You also could use touches of autumn green in the prints in that room, which could include yellow, orange, light blue, and a dash of pink. This sky-blue room could be accented throughout with touches of pink.

Three important principles should be at work in the color connections in your house: *similarity, continuity,* and *closure.*

The principle of *similarity* can best be seen in a living room filled with many items in many colors, styles, and shapes. If there is a similarity throughout of color, style, or shape, the room will look "together" no matter how widely apart each individual piece is placed. You can practice the principle of similarity with color by using similar hues or degrees of brightness. Similarity will create unity. If you have a large area you want to unify, you can use the principle of similarity. Many small objects and lamps, many chairs and tables, and many pictures and wall hangings in a large room can all share a similar feature of color, style, or shape. However far apart you put the similar items, they will continue to relate to the others and pull together as a perceptual unit.

Pastels will also relate to their primary colors. There is a pull among them that unifies more than the conscious mind is able to understand but that the unconscious color eye can appreciate. The effect of the message sent to the brain by your inner color eye is pleasing. Similarity is always a pleasing discovery, whether among like-minded people or in a room. Grouping like with like is always more harmonious than grouping widely differing items together.

The second color-connecting principle is *continuity.* Imagine what happens to a painting when you step back from it ten or twenty paces. The colors begin to merge and form a pleasing whole. When decorating an entire house, the overall statement is also made through the use of color. If there is no overall continuity to a home environment, if each room has a separate design and color scheme that does not relate to that overall identity, then the rooms will fracture the overall mood. People who live in such rooms will move from one to the other and find nothing that defines the *whole* house, only the parts. This can be more disconcerting than the conscious self recognizes.

However, if there is too much continuity, too much of an overall definition made of the whole, and if that aspect is allowed to dominate to too great a degree, then the result is boring and unexciting. In order to put excitement back into too much continuity, do the unpredictable now and then. Find one stunning antique and put it in a modern hallway. A modern home that has a cooled-out background like ecru can show off interesting period items. Whether that hall piece is an elaborately inlaid lacquered table or a prize Shaker bench, make sure that your focal point is a strong one. If your antiques are really reproductions, perhaps they shouldn't be given such importance.

The third principle of color connection is *closure.* When the mind's eye perceives a grouping, it has a need to complete it. For instance, if you see a card table with only three chairs around it, your mind's eye perceives a need for a fourth. This need to "finish off" applies to color because of the eye's need for contrast. In a room filled with warm colors, the eye seeks out the cool ones, as though thirsty for them. Similarly, in a room full of cool colors, the eye seeks out the warm ones. A warm color can look "hot" in a cool room simply by means of contrast. In a room without color, the eye searches for it among the monotony of black or beige.

Color on Woodwork and Trim

One of the things people do to add color to a room is to paint their woodwork bright colors like orange. But woodwork should not be painted hard, distracting colors like orange, green, dark brown, or bright red. I've even seen woodwork painted black or dark green and the walls a lighter or contrasting color. I never mind woodwork in what is called the Williamsburg colors, the soft beiges, the light blues, and the pale treen green, but woodwork to me is always meant to be a secondary element of a room. I never think a room is complete without crown molding between the wall and the ceiling, moldings around the doors, and detail around the windows, but I never like to see them a color. I think people paint their woodwork dark from a sense of practicality, so that they won't have to keep it up as much.

But when dark woodwork peels, it looks worse than if it had been painted a light color. I've known people who paint the woodwork different colors from room to room. One girl's room will have blue woodwork, the next girl's room pink, and another room orange. The practice is generally a disaster, particularly when the radiators as well as the radiator covers are painted the same color as the woodwork. The only time I like to draw attention to a radiator is in an old-fashioned house. I have painted old-fashioned radiators metallic gold or silver, and sometimes I've painted them bright red, because red indicates heat. In that case I think the use of contrasting color can be appropriate.

Color in the Hallway

What should you do with the halls of your home when it comes to color? This will never be a problem again if you plan your color scheme in a unifying way. The color of your halls is the first and most important question to consider in using color magic in your home. Why? Because the colors you select there will determine the colors that you use throughout the house.

Don't forget the impact of first impressions. An entrance hall should convey the spirit of the house: warm, open, sunny, formal, dramatic, serene, intimate, classic, avant-garde. Whatever the impression you want to create, it will be created here first. First impressions are more important than the rational side of us would like to think.

The secret of unifying color begins at the beginning, in the foyer. If you choose a wallpaper here, look for one that includes several of your favorite colors. You will unify your house by picking up one of those colors and using it somewhere in the living room. Unifying color is like a thread that unwinds throughout your house. Our color eye, which is forever seeking out continuity in color, picks up the color thread and is satisfied. The look is never boring, for your color choices can be varied and their uses subtle.

Many tests have been done on the response to color, and it's nearly all subliminal. What your color eye perceives becomes part of your general mood, the one you can't quite explain. Learning to satisfy your color eye's preferences will do much to provide a soothing, unifying, and always interesting atmosphere for your home. Fail to satisfy this inner eye and it can become jumpy and nervous. Where to land? it wants to know, and in that moment you've broken the mood that color continuity is supposed to provide.

Step into the room adjoining your living room, and your color eye should again fall on a familiar color. A dining-room chair may pick up the color of the living-room walls, or a painting can contain the color of the rug. From room to room this is how you carry the color thread along, adding one color that carries over to another room easily and pleasingly.

The Living Room in Color

The living room is the major color choice and the most difficult. The first problem to consider, even before color, is the amount of light. If too little light is the biggest problem in your living room, your color solution is to pick light, sunny colors and avoid deep, dark, grayed-out colors. Pick a sunny soft lemon, sky blue, fawn beige, or pale petal pink for the walls. In addition to the brightener on the walls, use bright fabrics in spring colors. This will take care of making your room more light and bright by day, but what about at night? Make sure that you have enough light sources in your living room to prevent it from becoming too dark then, too. You could put lights behind your drapery valances, sconces on the walls, or Colonial candles on many small tables.

If your living room does not have a light problem, then you are free to use those dramatic, rich, dark-colored walls that are so much in favor in all styles: English, with its use of mustard, hunting green, or the paneled wall; Oriental, with its saffron gold and red and black lacquer; Colonial, with its rich gray greens, slate blues, and muted yellows; and classic modern with its use of bright Mondrian primaries, Yves Saint Laurent's clear vivid winter colors, and, of course, the popular postmodern colors of dove, taupe, dusty rose, wine, and currant.

If you want to do your living room in the grayed-down, frosted postmodern colors, you almost have to have a bright and sunny room. At night, make sure that you have plenty of light sources in your room, because the postmodern colors do not reflect light. Use lights on the walls, in the corners of your room, behind the valances, on the low tables, high tables, and the backs of breakfronts. Use chandeliers on the ceiling or track lighting, for the postmodernists love the pinpoint look in lighting effects.

I like the dark-walled modern room with either chocolate-brown walls or deep hunter-green walls. If you like that kind of richly toned room, you might accent the walls with bright new spring colors, the green-green of new growth and fresh shoots. Use them with plenty of sunshine yellow and white. Remember that in a truly sunny room, the sun tones down the colors drastically. That's why bright colors don't fight one another in a sunny room.

Maybe your living room problem is ceiling height. Perhaps you live on the parlor floor of a typical brownstone or have a cathedral living room. Or perhaps you have a claustrophobic condo-height ceiling of eight feet. Let's consider the too-low ceiling first, because less can be done about it—very little in fact. You can paint it white or you can use a wallpaper with a strong vertical stripe to it. More can be done with color for a ceiling that is too high.

It's all very well to point out with pride to your guests that your brownstone ceiling is the traditional thirteen feet. But what does it feel like to live in such a room? You don't want to feel as though you're living in a museum when you're at home, or in an echo chamber. This feeling of lack of enclosure intensifies at night when no light reaches at all to the far recesses of your ceiling. This high-ceilinged room is hard to make cozy. If you want to cozy up your high ceiling, consider painting it a bright color like saffron yellow, which will gleam and reflect light from below. Lit properly, it might even look like gold gilt. You might paint your walls a cooled-down version of that same saffron, which will catch the sun as it travels from one side of your house to the other. Or you might send your ceiling out into infinity by giving it the French treatment with pink and white clouds on a pinky-blue ceiling. In that case, paint the trim white.

Suppose that you want your living room to reflect a particular mood. Maybe this is where you frequently entertain, or where you sit with people you don't know well enough to take into the family room or the kitchen. Or maybe it's a place where you want to be quiet and restful and have a cup of tea with your feet up. For whatever moods you want to achieve you can select an appropriate color.

If you are a winter person or a person who likes those strong but not hot colors and want a room that is conducive to a good party because you entertain a lot, then consider Yves Saint Laurent colors: dramatic Oriental black, snow white, Christmas red and green, and strong violet blue. These are not quiet colors, but they're not loud, either. If you're a partygiver, you only want quiet in such a room after guests depart, when you can reflect on the party with someone special.

But if your living room is a place for you to gather your wits about you with your feet up on the coffee table, Mozart on the tape deck, and a stack of reading material at your side, you may want to choose an all-linen look in neutral shades of beige. Or you might like a quiet dove-gray, banana-cream, pale sun-yellow, or serene sky-blue room. Here *restful* doesn't have to mean uninteresting, just toned down, the kind of room where there are no loud voices, a place to cool out from the rigors of life and talk quietly with loved ones.

Accents in this quiet living room will make a strong statement. Anything that you put in this restful beige room will make a much more assertive statement than it would in a bright and busy room. Like the jewel on the diamond merchant's black velvet, your accessories are on display in such a room, only more subtly, of course, than on dramatic jeweler black. Make sure that your accessories make a statement that you like. Fortunately, accents can be changed at will and at whim. Make a subdued statement one day, a whimsical one the next. The modern painting that made you ecstatic in the fall may be giving you heartburn by spring. No matter. Replace your accents with objects that reflect your current state of mind. It doesn't matter what objects you choose, as long as they harmonize well with each other, they will only be enhanced by the cool linen of your subdued background.

Living-room color also has to mix and match with a lot of different kinds of woods. Although the sofa is often fully upholstered, many other pieces of furniture in a living room are going to have their wood exposed: the side chairs, tables, end tables, coffee tables, pull-up chairs, and shelving. All these wood pieces need to harmonize. They do not, however, need to match, because tree colors do not clash but harmonize. Take a look at inlay for a good example of tree harmony. You can mix all sorts of woods and stains and styles and finishes in your living room. However, if you're dealing with a variety of wood colors in your living room, I would refrain from using a wide variety of color in wall, carpet, and fabric, as well, because that would be too confusing.

If you are a lover of wood, then begin with your orangey-pink whorled pine living-room floor and rub it with butcher's wax and a buffer. On that floor might be more pine furniture or furniture that is predominantly oak or mahogany. Perhaps you like your oak floor bleached so that the fine veins of its grain are exposed. Or maybe you like oak the way it was at Grandma's—dark and varnished once a year.

Maybe you have a mahogany- or ebony-colored piano in your living room that is the room's main color feature. Or maybe that piano is painted a high-gloss white enamel. Wood can make a major color statement in a room, which is why you must consider it first when you are planning living-room colors.

Pale blond wood is now in favor again in the woods of the Art Deco period and the 1950s revival. Bleached walnut, natural bamboo, wicker—the color range of the lighter-colored woods is easy to work with, especially in a room that needs light. There is also a revival of the popular lacquer finishes that come in the postmodern colors and not in wood colors at all. They, too, mix nicely with wood pieces.

When my predecessor, Dorothy Draper, came upon the scene shortly after World War II, she declared an end to drab. She soon had the entire country painting its woodwork gleaming white enamel. The woodwork in your home may still be painted that gleaming white. Unless you have returned to the original wood, gleaming white to banana cream is nearly always my choice for woodwork. Of course, if your predecessors managed to restrain themselves during the white-enamel-woodwork painting craze, then I suggest you take good care of your precious unpainted woodwork. If you give it a cleaning with a wax, it will continue to add luster and beauty to your living-room color scheme.

If you are a wood lover, be sure to choose a color for your walls that shows off your wood to its greatest advantage. Green is a good background color for wood, and by green I mean the deep forest greens in their wide variety of shades. Although I believe spring and summer greens complement the wood in your rooms, autumn colors are too strong. However, paled-down shades of orange, from whited pumpkin to apricot to peach, are beautiful shades to accompany pine. A dark-stained oak floor is enhanced by the company of banana cream or celadon or even a rich coral. Remember to think of the wood in your living room when contemplating a new color there. Observe each piece and consider how you can draw them all together with the color of your carpet and of your walls.

Here is a Southwestern living room in the style inspired by that great artist Georgia O'Keeffe. It would look gorgeous in Phoenix or Santa Fe. There are many shades of brown that are luscious in the Southwestern setting that would be too dry and barren to use anywhere else. There's a barrenness about this countryside that people live with all the time, so it is appropriate to bring into the home environment those dry colors from outside: clay brown, beige, sage green, and a bit of the Southwestern blue sky. When planning a Southwestern living room, begin with a sand-colored carpet. If you choose a shag, you might try brown, or copper, or beige. Put a brown sofa against a sand-colored wall and accent that sofa with big woven Indian pillows in rust. A sage green and beige print pillow could be used, too.

On the floor, on top of the beige shag rug, might be a beige and orange geometric design in an Indian weave. The design should be open and have a border. There might be just a touch of Southwestern blue sky in it, too. For chairs in this room, I would select large-scale furniture that is wide and deep. Hassocks could be covered in natural hide. There could be a lot of pottery filled with cactus or sage. In a connecting dining room in the open style of the Southwestern house, there could be a cool tile floor. The walls could be the same sand color as the living room, although the ceiling could be painted in a bright yellow, a touch softer than primary yellow. People who like the modern feeling might be tempted to try a bittersweet or clay-orange ceiling. Desert dining chairs could be fully upholstered in wheat with brown stained legs.

Perhaps you see your living room as a tranquil place with a Continental accent. Here is a traditional English room in a frosted mint green. The panels could be painted in a clear frosted mint and the molding a chalk white. Between the moldings and the panels on the wall could be a pretty light creamy beige area. Because it's an English room, there would be a big, chalk-white crown molding around the room. I would paint the ceiling the same cream beige as the area between the wall panels.

For a carpet, I would choose a loop done in an English petit point manner. The basic color could be a soft cream beige, and there might be a pattern of green crisscrossing branches. For upholstery in the room I would select two round-backed chairs with pretty skirts and a sofa also with a rounded back. I would upholster them in raw silk in the same mint green that is on the walls. For pillow accents and throw pillows, I would pick an azalea pink and a green-and-white striped fabric. I would use a painted tray table in black and gold with a floral design painted onto the papier-mâché of the tray. This would sit in front of the fireplace for use by people on the sofa as well as people seated on the two pull-up chairs. Between those two chairs you need a small table. I would use an attractive English step table that has beige leather panels with blind tooling on each of the steps.

I would choose a brass or gold-tinted standing lamp with a big shade in a natural color silk and would line this shade in a flesh tone. I always line my lampshades with a color, because a natural skin-tone lining or even a pink lining in the shade will improve the quality of light in the room. When the light is off, you can't see the color, but when the light is on, the tinted inside of the lampshade can add color to the room. For instance, if I have a peach room, I use a peach silk-stocking color to line the inside of the shade and take away the stark white look of the light bulb against the white shade. There's nothing more discordant than coming into a room to find the light so white and hard that it takes away all the subtleties of the objects it illuminates. Sometimes I line my opaque shades with a gold crackle so that when you look over the top or come down the stairs into a room you're looking into a golden glow.

In this English room I would line the room with family portraits or horse prints in burled wood frames hung in groupings. Another touch of green I would use in the room is a desk chair covered in green-and-white cut velvet. I would choose an old-fashioned geometric design on a Queen Anne–style chair to pull up to a good looking flat writing table.

Dining Room Color

In all my decorating experience, no room ends up winning the dreariness award more often than the dining room. I don't know why this room is so often a color disaster, but then again I have never understood the concept that dining should be a somber event. I believe that the dining room should have but one focus: appetite. Rather than having a dining room filled with a lot of collectibles gathering dust, I prefer a dining room that is set up for the sole purpose of stimulating the appetite, where every object on display pertains to the purpose of dining. I prefer as a focus in a dining room a large splendid platter on a hutch lit by a lamp at night to a shelf full of porcelain lords and ladies.

If you eliminate all objects in your dining room unrelated to the process of eating, you will already have unified your dining room by merely taking things away. You might also consider that other unifier: color. Scientific researchers report that orange, pale yellow, vermilion, pale green, pale brown, and dark brown stimulate the appetite. I recommend approaching these appetite-stimulating colors not in their usual paint-box shades but in more sophisticated food shades.

Grade-school orange may stimulate the appetite on an unconscious level, but the sophisticated color-conscious part of you might reject it as too reminiscent of Halloween. Fortunately, there are many other shades to choose from. There's flaming red orange, which is delicious in a Chinese lacquer. Then there's spicy cinnabar, juicy kumquat, or, closer to home, sunny Florida orange. There are the rich varieties of whited-out oranges, all guaranteed appetite stimulators. Consider the cool orange shade of the inside of a pumpkin, like a pumpkin soufflé, or the shade of the skin of a rosy-blushed nectarine. There's also pinkish salmon and golden peach. All of the orange family is vibrant and exciting. Mixed with white, the appetite-stimulating qualities of these oranges can be cooled out, like adding a creamy béchamel sauce to that pumpkin soufflé.

Light green is another appetite stimulator and therefore another popular dining-room choice. There's lettuce green, pale, elegant French celadon green, originally a jade color from the Far East, and the more lively creamed-asparagus green. All these light greens get the saliva flowing. Another color that does the same thing is pale yellow, not the strong acid yellow of the primary paint box but the yellow in homemade lemon pie. This cooled-out lemon is a clear but pale color, yet it's still vibrant. I also like the pale yellow of pineapple, apricot, and banana cream. These yellows have been popular dining-room color choices among my clients over the years.

Brown is a color that evokes a sensory response in the taste buds. It is the color of crisply baked turkey and chocolate mousse, toffee and cappuccino, rich beef gravy and Black Forest cake. I like the combination of coffee and cream in a dining room, or chocolate and mocha, doubling your sensory enjoyment, for studies indicate that both light brown and dark brown are colors that stimulate the appetite.

Obviously, within the wide range of these proven appetite-stimulating colors, there is much to choose from. What you choose will depend on the light and your individual preferences, the dining-room style you want, the scale of the room, and what kind of accessories you have. If, for instance, you have traditional mahogany furniture in your dining room, your walls could take the brightening-up effect of lemon with a white ceiling and trim. Or you might try a lemon-and-white-patterned wall covering.

A modern dining room should have a clean and clear look to the colors. Choose among vivid winter blue-green shades and accents, dense and vivid lemon yellow, emerald green, or shocking pink to shine along with clear glass and chrome. To me, the dining room is a place for clarity in colors and line.

Maybe your dining room is formal in character with fancy molding and panels. I say go all the way with that look. Use a beige moiré on the walls and brown velvet on the dining chairs and hang precious paintings on the walls.

Vermilion red is another of the appetite-stimulating colors. If you like crystal, there's nothing that shows it off better in a dining room than red walls in an Empire style. You might like to use big black and gold, Empire-style chairs. They can be covered in a fern green or black satin to glow against those red walls. I would set the table with a delicate gold-banded china, because there's so much going on in the room itself. Fine white china would provide light in that darkly handsome red room and would further enhance the light from the crystal fixtures.

In another dining room with red walls, I might hang big tapestries on the wall. Ideally, this room would have big baronial molding over the doors. It could also have a Spanish feeling, given large wrought-iron fixtures and candelabra. It might have host and hostess chairs, but I prefer a table where all the chairs have arms. This is also the kind of room that could have wide-board floors and lots of candlelight from big torches and large metal candelabra.

Another important way color enters the dining picture is in the linen, the placemats, the china, the glassware, the centerpiece, and in the jewelry of the dining room, the silverware. These items should be thought of as part of the overall color picture whose only statement is bon appetit.

A common feature of dining areas in houses in the southern parts of the country is their proximity to the out-of-doors. In a more northern climate, this kind of room might have screens in the summer or sliding glass doors. I suggest decorating such a dining room with carefully selected colors from nature. You might choose spring greens, full-bodied summer greens, old-fashioned garden colors, autumn colors, or the sun-washed pastels and aquamarine colors of the seaside. Whatever season or climate you use as inspiration for your dining-room color palette, make sure to include lots of light. If your dining room doesn't have lots of natural light, then use plenty of the two color substitutes for light: white and pale yellow. However, at night, do not overlight a dining room. People are uncomfortable dining in a room that is too bright. They don't meet each other's eyes in such a setting. Lower the lights, ideally to candlelight level, and people will relax and enjoy themselves.

For dining areas that are as much out-of-doors as in, I include the look of nature in the composition of the floor and the furnishings. I like the use of brick or stone underfoot in a dining area open to the out-of-doors, softened with small, soft cotton rugs in pale colors. I like straw mats on the table, and lots of wicker and plants. Pillows in such a room can be floral splashes. When dining rooms are this close to nature, you almost have to go natural in your color choice, because the natural world has a way of making our latest fad look foolish. I particularly dislike the look of grayed-out postmodern colors in a dining room, especially in close proximity to nature. They may be today's trend, but my appetite is not stimulated by gray food. The advertising and packaging researchers will tell you that gray communicates a weak, old, and enervated feeling. None of these connotations stimulates the appetite. Maybe if I planned to go on a diet over a long period of time, I would choose a dove-gray wall for my dining room or a dusty rose, an acid puce, a taupe, or an aniline mauve, because none of these colors is associated in my mind with food. In such a dining room, surrounded by such colors, I would probably lose weight.

For a dining room in primary Chinese yellow begin with saffron-yellow lacquered walls. The baseboards and chair rails and moldings could all be painted black lacquer with a metallic gold trim. The dining-room rug could be a Chinese design in black, mustard yellow, and cinnabar red. The dining table could be glass with a bronze doré frame and a Chinese fretwork base. The chairs could have simple lines in black lacquered wood. The seats could have cushions covered in yellow fabric with a Chinese coin design and tied on with fringed silk cords. In the center of the table might be a big, black, lacquered Oriental bowl. The water glasses could be bronze and long-stemmed in a Far Eastern design. The table could be set with straw placemats. On one of the yellow walls could be a beautiful Chinese Coromandel screen. Lighting would be provided by downlights, not a chandelier. This Oriental dining room is primarily in yellow pulled together with the black and gold trim. The ceiling could also be metallic gold.

Another color I believe in staying away from in a dining room is blue. Blue may be everybody's favorite color in china, but an all-blue wall or an all-blue carpet is too cool and serene for the act of dining. Very little blue food exists and lots of blue in a dining room is not a way to get the gustatory juices flowing. The darker shades especially have a tendency to make the eye go off into infinity. What you want in the dining room is concentration on the here and now, not contemplation of the infinite. What would be good in, say, a den or library will not work with food, and whatever color doesn't work well with food you want to leave out of your dining room.

If your dining room is not really a room but an area off the living room between it and the kitchen, you have a special dining problem. You can enlarge the area by putting sheet mirrors on the wall, and then you can enclose the area with color. Don't close it off completely, however. For the sake of unity pick up a color from the living room and use it in the dining area. Don't be talked into a matching look, however. The salesman at the furniture store might try to convince you to buy a matching living-room and dining-room set, but I suggest you resist. The look would be overcoordinated and dull, dull, dull.

Today's color palette, like the cuisine, is showing a definite tilt to the East where the manner of dining is above all serene, a conscious, artful, and unhurried act prepared with much thought for the stimulation of all the senses. The Oriental dining room is scaled down not in size but in the number of visible objects. Only eating utensils are in view. Bowls, cups, and chopsticks (which are silent compared to Western silverware) are objects to admire. Walls are an appetite-stimulating rich dark brown lacquer, the brown of Coromandel, spicy vermilion, or glowing saffron. In such a room, how could the taste buds fail to be stimulated?

The Kitchen

When it comes to color in the kitchen, the same rules for appetite-stimulating colors apply, for in most homes as much eating is done in the kitchen as in the dining room, and the eating done there is of the most intimate and day-to-day kind. However, some colors that enhance the appetite are those that might not be suitable for a room dedicated to the task of preparing food and cleaning up afterward. A lot of serious cooks deplore the use of fancy wallpaper in kitchens, or tasseled curtains, or intricate molding on the cupboard doors. They see the kitchen as a work area that they want to be clean, uncluttered, and convenient. Of course, food preparation must be done in a clean kitchen. The more things you have exposed in a kitchen, the more dust and grease will collect. Over the years I have noticed that it is the serious cook who wants to have her or his implements easily within reach and even within view, depending on the look of the object. It is the dilettante cook who will hang a series of fruit-and-flower prints on the kitchen wall. It is the serious cook who likes to work in a kitchen big enough for an assistant but not so big that he or she has to do a lot of walking back and forth. It is the dilettante cook who wants a kitchen that has the width of a football field.

What we are really talking about is background color. What color are those walls that will be filled with the practical things needed by a good cook with a varied repertoire going to be? In a kitchen, the background color becomes the ground, and the tools of food preparation become the figures. Obviously, if you want to display these implements as figure-on-ground, they need to be of good design. Fortunately, a lot of kitchenware these days is well designed. Much antique cookware was made to last. It is also plentiful, especially the treasured bowls, crockery, and glass jars of the past one hundred years.

In no room does nostalgia ring as loud and clear as in the kitchen. Given the opportunity and the budget, most people would end up in the kitchen of their grandparents, redolent with the spicy smell of gingerbread. If you want this sort of old-fashioned cluttered look, then choose a background color taking light into consideration. This color should be cheerful and strong, but not on the dark side. The kitchen is not a place for powdered pastels, but for well-defined natural food colors, not grayed but a shade lighter than you might find in your garden. If you have a colorful collection of kitchenware including lots of copper, consider painting your kitchen walls appetite-stimulating apple green, spiced pumpkin, mango, espresso brown, or maybe a rich salmon.

Some people don't like to cook in a cluttered-looking kitchen. They like to put their things away behind doors and in drawers, and keep their spaces open and bare. They think the look of a kitchen at its busiest is as untidy as they can tolerate. Cooking amid a jumble of hanging pots, herbs, onions, and glass jars of pasta is not their way. For them I suggest cupboards with glass doors and a vivid pattern of leaves and sumptuous berries on the walls. Behind the glass cupboard doors can be lights that illuminate from above pretty kitchen things on glass shelves. This way it is possible to have a little display and tucked-away order at the same time.

An important color element to consider in your kitchen spectrum is wood. To me, the more wood in a kitchen the better, because the look of food and wood together is a natural. Who knows for how long people have been eating from slabs of wood? I should imagine almost forever. To me, a kitchen without a wood table lacks something essential. In my own kitchen, the wood table is where the most important activity goes on—the daily business of family living. Along with that wood table, there's also wood in the cupboards, wooden bowls, wood in the butcher-block counters, and wood in the shutters at the window. I am especially fond of the faded patina of old well-scrubbed wood when it develops that silver-brown quality so admired by wood lovers as well as lovers of the color brown. In the cosmetic categories of color, that silvery brown of much-bleached and much-washed wood falls into the summer range. From the bleached kitchen pine in the light brown spectrum to the dark brown of stained oak and pine, wood also falls into the category of the appetite-stimulating colors and wood adapts to almost every style with ease. I love knotty pine in a country kitchen and I love French kitchens with painted wood walls and bleached wood floors. I like lots of green with this wood, especially in the form of plants, herbs in a window-box, or a column of ivy growing up an interior brick wall.

If your kitchen adjoins your dining room or dining area, it should be easy to find a similar color in your dining room to carry over into the kitchen to unify the two rooms or areas. You might pick up the orange in a dining-room seat cushion or the light cocoa in a dining-room rug and use that color in the kitchen. That way, every time people move between those two rooms, as they do frequently, their inner color eye will be able to distinguish similarities between them and will not get restless.

One thing I've learned to avoid over the years is the use of too many dark colors in the kitchen. If you have a lot of dark wood, lighten it up with blue, yellow, or green in the paler shades. Paint the ceiling and trim a bright reflecting white and cover the chairs in a bright, spicy color like tangerine, saffron, or tomato red.

Another common kitchen color problem is what to do with the old avocado or coppertone kitchen appliances. Don't despair. Use fresh green, cool melon, hot pink, and lots of white. A combination of those colors in a floral or geometric pattern will brighten up those dull, once trendy, and now troublesome colors.

The Family Room in Color

Family-room colors are limited to those deemed "practical," unless, of course, you like to worry and make your family feel uncomfortable. The family room is not the place for the pastel rug or the silk celadon sofa. A better way to cover an aging sofa would be in a strong, rich color like navy, hunter green, or burgundy and in a tough fabric like canvas, duck, denim, or linen. I find that family-room couches slipcovered in a natural fabric that is frequently washed develop character. The colors soften and marry and mutate slightly over the years. Like an old friend, such a couch fabric ages well along with you.

It is the custom among the British upper classes to be extremely reluctant to part with old slipcovers, even after they begin to reveal a bit of chair leg because of shrinkage from constant cleaning. Do the high-born British mind? They do not. They enjoy the patina of that old fabric, and a view of chair legs seems a small price to pay. If you choose the same kind of quality fabric in a traditional pattern, you may one day face the same dilemma when your humble sofa's well-washed nubby linen must finally be replaced.

Other colors and fibers in the family room should be chosen with the same care that you devote to choosing couch fabric and color. They should be able to recover from a spill and take a lot of sun and normal wear and tear. Family-room colors should be on the warm side, but not too hot. You don't want too much stimulation from the colors, but you don't want cool colors either. Remember that the family room is for relaxing and relating to other family members and friends. Family-room colors should be warm and unifying and I like covering several pieces of family room furniture in the same fabric. The color choice might be a rich burgundy, a ruddy raspberry, or a deep purple and green print. Against this furniture, I would place pillows in gay colors with lots of white accents.

The Bedroom in Color

Bedroom color should be a world apart from the wide-awake downstairs colors. Bedrooms are the place where personal color preference really shows. People tend to paint their bedrooms in more unusual and intimate colors than the ones they use in their more public rooms. They choose fanciful shades of the purple family like mauve, lilac, and soft lavender or they choose exotic colors like persimmon or deep aquamarine. Some people don't go in for fanciful colors as much as bright ones, because they think of their bedrooms as places to wake up in. These people want to be sung awake with cheerful colors. Often they choose to live in bedrooms full of sunny country-garden colors. Other people don't think of their bedrooms as a place to wake up in but as a late-night retreat where they may spend important time relaxing, reading, writing, watching television, or being with a special someone. That kind of room is toned down in terms of color. Bright and cheerful morning moods are too intense for a nighttime look in the bedroom. Evening colors such as pale blue and jade green have a serene quality. Whether cool, warm, soft, or loud you can establish any mood you want through color.

The basis for choice in the bedroom begins in infancy. From what we know about early perception of color, children of a very young age can't even perceive secondary colors, let alone whited-out pastels. The last colors that should be used in an infant's room are pink and blue. The stimulation they receive from these colors is a minus rather than a plus, because infants can't bear the feeling of being in a void. They like to feel enclosed, the way they felt in their womb days when everything was warm and cozy. If you want your infant to feel enclosed, avoid pastels. Infants' rooms should be full of light and gay colors, and those colors should be in the clear and primary state. No fooling around with hues, please, in the infant's room! It will only confuse the baby.

Nor would you want to provide too much stimulation in the background color in an infant's room. What stimulates the baby are bits of moving colors in toys and light. If you paint the baby's walls primary red or yellow, the poor thing might become overstimulated because of the figure-and-ground effect. You don't want brightness in both the background and the pattern of the baby's toys. Besides, if you paint the baby's walls primary red or yellow, they become dark at night, almost black, and a too-dark room is not good for the baby either.

I like a neutral color for the walls, one that's there strictly for background, like white or cream, against which the baby's growing collection of toys and games can be placed. Reflecting light from the walls will make the environment sunny and cheerful, even when there is no sun. I might use a big colorful floating balloon pattern in the wallpaper, or animals or apple trees, all large scale. Babies can't perceive small objects from a distance, but they can see big, bright objects in a wallpaper. With such surroundings, the baby will feel enclosed in happy colors and familiar objects.

Babies spend a lot of time in their room. If the room is too empty or too uninviting, the baby's world is sad and under-stimulated. But if a room is bright and cheerful and the baby associates it with happy play, then the environment provides just the right degree of stimulation. I recommend the introduction of color into a baby's life where the baby spends most of the time—on the rug. A colorful rug becomes a play area. Rather than wall-to-wall carpet, I would use area rugs, or rugs on top of rugs. These rugs can be squares and circles, which should have borders of contrasting colors. Then the baby can literally feel blue and red and orange and yellow and green, crawling from color to color, and can become intimately as-sociated with these astonishing differences as he or she begins to develop color perception. Imagine the fascination of watch-ing a new color gradually come into focus. And to think people wonder what it is that babies find so fascinating about color! One of the wonderful things about raising children is watching them make discoveries for the first time, and one of the earliest and most meaningful discoveries children make is the discov-ery of color. You can help the process along and sharpen your child's sense of color as it develops.

As a baby grows into a toddler and then into a child who

is able to go outside and play, the room loses its importance as a total environment. Out of doors, children learn about nature and other children. They exercise their muscles, run and shout and climb trees, and play themselves into a state of famished exhaustion. Then they come home, eat, and go to a room that you may prefer not to think about, so untidy and disgusting a sight is it. One of the most discouraging aspects of the typical child's room is its chaos. Nothing has a place. There is no way the average child has the ability, let alone the motivation, to make order out of such chaos. You, dear parent, need to help, and to assist you, there is color.

Here is how to bring order into your child's room with color. First, there needs to be a unifying background color. This is no place for busy wallpaper or cutesy curtains. Your child probably has too much visual distraction in that room already, as most children need to be surrounded by a lot of "stuff."

Ask your child what color walls and carpet he or she prefers, and then fulfill that request. It is most likely not going to be too bizarre. I find that children of six to twelve are not interested in displays of the unique or the eccentric. That comes later. Most likely your child's choice is going to be red or blue. The rug should be a lighter shade of the same color as the walls. For instance, you could use red lacquer on the walls of a boy's room and a red-and-brown-flecked tweed rug. Off-setting the sky-blue walls of a girl's room could be an Oriental carpet in navy, pale blue, and beige.

Bedcovers in a child's room should be simplified. Why should making a bed be a big deal? Given a choice, most children prefer a sleeping bag on top of the sheets. Just use a fitted sheet on the bed with some matching pillows. In the morning, pajamas can be stuffed into the sleeping bag and rolled up at the end of the bed. You can skirt that bed with more of the same sheeting or use a navy or deep red.

In order to establish a color-coded filing system in your

child's room, take your cue from the child's own color preferences. Select six favorites and then let him or her decide what
colors to assign to the different categories of clothing, toys, art
and craft supplies, and sporting equipment needed. For instance, your child might select red for winter clothes, blue for
summer clothes, green for sporting equipment, yellow for
games, purple for collections of cars, airplanes, soldiers, and
other small items, pink for dolls and doll clothes. At once your
child will begin to understand that putting like things together
in a room makes it much easier to retrieve them. This is often
the motivating factor in restoring and maintaining order in a
child's room. The best way to maintain that order is on a daily
basis. Maybe you can schedule your own straightening-up
time to correspond with that of your child. A color-coded
method is also soothing to a child, because it is nonverbal.
Pretty soon a child will feel uncomfortable putting a winter
sweater in a summer drawer. Restoring order to a child's room
can be satisfying to all concerned. It provides a sense of peace
and serenity to you and your child, and it's one less thing to
fight about. The child feels in control of his or her own environment, rather than being enslaved to the constant task of
finding things.

Since time immemorial, blue has been the color relegated
to boys. Boyhood rites of passage are the blue bassinet with the
blue bow, the navy-blue school blazer, and then graduation to
the blue business suit. And so it is that men are locked into
blue for life, because it is supposed to be *the* male color. It will
probably surprise no one to hear that blue is also the color most
men say they prefer. They prefer blue in their rooms as they
do in their clothing.

To decorate a blue room for a boy, Colonial style, start
with the bunching pieces common to Colonial times, where
everything fits together. A chest connects to a desk that has
shelves above it, and next to it are bunching chests-on-chests.

For some reason boys like this kind of furniture. Maybe it makes them feel they are fortified against the world. There are also matching night tables and matching headboards available. Not only can you buy these bunching chests for boys with beds to match, you can get them with the bunk and trundle beds that boys love. There's something that appeals to boys about sleeping high up, and they also like the feature of one bed sliding under another to make more room for roughhousing.

Here is a boy's room designed around a bunching unit in Colonial blue. In such a room, the carpet would be red, or navy, or a red, white, and blue plaid. The walls could be soldier-boy red. There's something macho about this room, more military and conformist in influence than many mothers would like. However, being the father of three boys, I know that little boys are into soldiers and cowboys and *Star Wars*. Later on they might learn to like the Grateful Dead or Boy George and begin to express less hidebound tastes, but young boys just want a room that feels like a fort, that feels as familiar to them as their old jeans. At this age boys are great traditionalists, so why not give them their blue and red and be done with it?

As your son becomes a little more fashionable, you might interest him in something washable with a shine to it, such as blue patent vinyl for the walls. Or you might paint the walls royal blue and give them a texture. Or you might think of using a blue and white ticking stripe. Another choice is a skipper blue and red geometric, provided you don't plan to keep the red-white-and-blue-plaid carpet. For lamps, boys like wooden-Indian lamp bases or fire-engine lamp bases. This boy's room is a formula room, no doubt about it, but it's a room that boys themselves like just because of the familiarity of the clichés.

Here's a scheme for a primary look in a little girl's room. Paint the walls yellow. For the curtains, find a print of red and yellow flowers tied with a blue bow (the stems of the flowers can be a soft black) and edge this in a soft yellow and white stripe. Paint all the furniture white with yellow trim. Use the striped fabric in the bedskirt. The bedspreads can be white with yellow throw pillows. The carpet can also be white.

The bedroom of the older child, from adolescence to the age when they leave the nest, is a far different environment from the young child's room where one's major concern is maintaining at least minimal order and cleanliness. The teen-ager's room is apt to be a den of self-expression, a place for rebellion against the uptight standards of the parents. I think this bedroom is a good place for the venting of a little harmless rebellion in the choice of color and design, as long as no permanent damage is done to the structure. Then the teen-ager will feel in control of at least a small area inside of which privacy is sacred. I believe as long as family hygiene standards are maintained in that room, and as long as other house rules are kept regarding what is allowed in the privacy of that room, the teen-ager should be allowed to dissent from the overall color scheme of your house and do his or her own thing. He or she should be allowed to go through the same fads and phases adults go through in their own quarters. It's just that adolescent phases are more intense as is adolescent color preference. Be thankful for doors. As long as you don't have to look at those colors, you shouldn't mind them.

Down the hall from the children is the private headquarters of the adult members of the family. Their bedroom needs to be a place for peace and quiet and intimate activities. Nothing in this environment need pertain to the needs of anyone besides its occupants. Nothing is more private than one's bedroom, and that privacy is often reflected in the colors people favor in them. Color preference in the bedroom may be too private a matter to reveal except to an intimate. Bedroom colors are often likely to be romantic, sometimes unabashedly so. The mood they create might be medieval, or Victorian, or lavishly French. But bedroom colors shouldn't be too stimulating. Remember that stimulating colors need light, and most bedrooms are used more by night than by day.

The bed of the master bedroom is the focal point of the room, and should make a major color statement. The bedskirt should be considered in the overall color scheme, as should the draperies at the window, the fabric on the side chair, and the sheets. A color-coordinated bedroom is easy these days. Deep, rich, wonderful colors now appear in sheet departments where once every color had a slightly washed-out look. Now you can use vivid colors on your bed, and these vivid shades might become the first choice you make in determining the colors in your bedroom palette. What colors are in the pattern of that gorgeous set of museum-reproduction sheets you are planning to buy? Along with the beige ground and the roses entwined with bright green leaves there might be black and brown birds with orange beaks and splashes of white. That's an ideal color palette for a cooled-down bedroom.

Here is a more lively bedroom for someone who wants to wake up cheerfully stimulated. It features strong primary colors and is in the classic American-modern style. Paint the walls paint-box blue and add a carpet and sofa in the same color. Accent that sofa with eighteen-inch pillows in yellow, red, and white. Give the pillows fully tucked Turkish corners. Bring in a steel-and-glass coffee table and use lacquered blue end tables and lamps. A club chair and ottoman can be upholstered in primary red and at the windows you can use white curtains trimmed in paint-box blue hung on navy-blue poles.

Mondrian was a painter who used brilliant primary colors in various combinations. Here is a master bedroom in Mondrian colors. Paint the walls paint-box yellow and the ceiling red. For an Oriental feeling, buy bamboo furniture and paint it all in red lacquer. Make the bedspreads bright yellow with bright red piping. Accent those bedspreads with bright blue pillows. Buy a beautiful paint-box blue lamp for the night table shaded in white with blue-and-red trim. On the wall behind the headboards you could hang a big modern painting in primary colors. On the floor could be black and white tiles.

Here is a pastel room done in melon for the country way of life. Melon is a good country color, and I like to think of it in terms of harvest pumpkin. This pastel pumpkin is whited down to look like the inside of the pumpkin. It goes very well with country pine furniture. I would find a cannonball pine bed that would go with the melon-colored walls. In a room that has dormers, as many upstairs country bedrooms do, I would use pine shutters at the windows. On the floor, preferably of twelve-to-fourteen-inch wide-board pine, you could lay a melon-white-and-wheat-colored cotton rug. At the entrance to the room, there might be a beautiful antique Americana hooked rug bordered in melon and black and featuring a melon-colored cat.

The furniture in the room would include a small American country chair with a cushion in a small melon-and-beige check. There could be pine country chests about the room, including a small pine washstand with a handsome white porcelain pitcher in a bowl resting on it. On the walls could be a series of prints, paintings, and needlepoint of country cats all framed differently. On the bed could be a white American country wedding quilt. The bed could be accented with pillows made out of an old soft blue and white quilt. The pillows are the one dash of color in this melon room, and even that dash of color is a faded, washed-out blue.

For a tranquil city or suburban room here's a one-color scheme in yellow. I would paper the walls in a soft yellow stripe. All the trim should be white. I would paint the ceiling yellow also. The soft carpet could be a beautiful pale yellow.

The bedclothing could be all white: a white bedskirt, white square canopy, and white side curtains. I'd add a dash of color in the white sheets by giving them a yellow edge or perhaps an orange flower with a little green trim in the pattern.

I would use French provincial furniture painted yellow, or I would choose a French Louis XV chair painted yellow with white trim. I would also use a small wood-frame bench painted yellow with white trim. I would upholster all this furniture in yellow and use a big white armoire with yellow trim. The armoire could have white doors on the inside and a big, beautiful key on the outside to which I would attach a French tassel. I have found that if there's an attractive tassel on the end of a key, you always know where it is.

Night tables in this yellow room could be white. Lamps could be white opaline with a spray of yellow flowers with a little pink and orange. The shades could be all white and trimmed in melon. This is the kind of room where you could use an oil painting in a gold frame, perhaps depicting one yellow rose against a forest green background. At the windows I would hang balloon shades. I would like the inset of the shade a pretty yellow, somewhat softer than the yellow on the fabrics of the bench and the chair.

Color in the Bathroom

Even people who paint all the rest of their walls white will want to paint their bathroom walls a color. The color spectrum for the bath has changed dramatically over the past few years, and fortunately that change has been for the better. There used to be a time when there were five standard bathroom colors: tan, mint, yellow, pink, and blue. None of them was inspiring from a decorating point of view. Similarly, there was a lack of imagination in bathroom wall covering, where powder pink and blue predominated for years.

Now the bathroom has become a place to make a major color statement. Beyond the usual boring pastels, there is now gleaming malachite, deep aubergine, and bright topaz. The new bathroom colors are the Old World mineral colors, and how they gleam. The gemstone colors have become popular for use in bathroom fixtures, too. These jewellike objects glitter and shine. The American bathroom has become sophisticated, indeed.

In this age of holistic health and athletic narcissism, the modern bathroom has become an especially important room. It is a room to look good in, which is why I think it's a smart idea to color your bathroom cosmetically. Selecting colors for your bathroom that enhance your skin tones is important when there are a lot of mirrors in your bath reflecting a lot of bare skin. When I did Joan Crawford's rooms, she always insisted on the harsh white light of day in her bathroom so that she would have no illusions about what she looked like in daylight. I think that's a rather severe attitude and that you should select bathroom colors that correspond to the cosmetic seasons. Winter people can have their dramatic black tile baths with vivid accents in towels and walls of emerald green, turquoise, and snow white. Winter jewelry in bathroom fixtures is ivory, silver, and crystal. Choose dramatic accents of good quality. A few exquisite pieces are better in a winter-color bath than a lot of cheaper ones. This is the bath that should glitter with a diamond brilliance.

Spring people can have hibiscus or seafoam green walls with accents of apricot, lilac, and peacock blue. Spring jewelry is pearl. Use lots of pearl in your cosmetically coordinated bath, as well as opal, emerald, and pale yellow gold. Fixtures should be on the delicate side and not too ornate.

Summer people can use pink in their baths, or lavender,

blue, or plum. The postmodern colors also look good in the bathroom done in summer shades. The summer jewelry is garnet or pink sapphire. Silver and platinum predominate. There is no gold.

Autumn is the place for gold. Autumn colors can be used lavishly in a complexion-coordinated bath. Choose coffee tile, desert-orange towels, and terra-cotta for the floor, with accents of caramel and oyster white. Jewelry for the bath done in autumn colors should be solid and substantial, not of the delicate variety. Fixtures can be ornamental gold, gleaming copper, amber, or topaz. Remember that gems are fired by autumn colors. Fortunately, the choice of bathroom fixtures in the gem category is wide. Tortoiseshell also complements the autumn bath.

Here is a bathroom in a color of raspberry I always associate with the French style. It is very flattering to most women. The shade of raspberry belongs to Madame Du Barry, and it is a delicate shade without too much white in it. I would use a raspberry silk moiré wallpaper with a border of white-and-gold rope featuring bouquets of raspberry-colored flowers with green leaves. In that border there might also be a dash of Mediterranean blue. I would paint the ceiling the same blue. On the floor I would use a wall-to-wall carpet in raspberry cotton and give it a finished border so that it could be taken up for cleaning.

The tub in this raspberry bathroom should be white, as should be the shower curtain. I would choose white silk draperies with a raspberry-colored fringe border and a waterproof liner. I would use big gold faucets and raspberry-colored towels initialed in aqua blue. I would also have a wastebasket of raspberry moiré and white with gold and clear crystal bathroom accessories. I would find pretty French period fashion prints in gold frames. The ladies would be wearing blue hats and the pictures would be hung from raspberry-colored ribbons.

Exterior Colors

There's a tradition of manor-house painting in America and for some reason that manor is painted white with green shutters. Someone once asked me, "Why do you think rich people all paint their houses white with green trim?" I don't know the answer, but it would seem that the grand white house with dark green shutters is still the ultimate status symbol to most people.

In Colonial times, barns were always painted red, because that color represented work buildings. But the master's house was always painted white with green trim. What would happen if you painted that white house with red shutters or with royal blue shutters? Most people would feel uncomfortable with such choices. I do like gray houses with white shutters, especially in coastal areas.

The approach to exterior color is different from that to interior color. When colors stand out against their environment or are abrasive, I think there's something wrong with them. For instance, buildings near beaches should have a feeling of the native woods and of the trees around them. If they must be concrete or cinderblock, I think they should be sand-colored or a soft brown gray that fits in with the landscape, so they don't look startling. Like most people, I am a traditionalist when it comes to exterior color. I advocate staying away from the bizarre.

What is more jarring during a drive through beautiful countryside than the sight of a house painted in stomach-medicine pink? Who knows what prompts people to paint their houses this ghastly pink? Unless you live in a place like Bermuda or Palm Beach, Florida, I believe in staying away from exterior pink. Actually I believe in staying away from pastels, period. There is just too much chance of conflict with environmental color. I believe that you should let the complexion of your house be determined by its surrounding environment. I don't believe houses should ever fight for attention with nature because the house will always lose.

In the urban setting, there's another problem. If you live in the city next to a neighbor who has just painted his house brick pink, don't be mean and paint your house acid green or brown. Both houses will look the worse for it. Just as in the country where houses shouldn't clash with nature, in the city they shouldn't clash with each other. That is why I believe there are so many white houses with green shutters. No matter what the environment, and no matter what the color of your neighbor's house, these colors will look good against the earth and sky and in the human community. A white house with green shutters is such a pleasing combination that driving down a road I often wonder what it would be like to live in one or another of them. I rarely dream about wanting to live in a yellow house with brown shutters, no matter how attractive the property, or (shudder) an avocado house with orange shutters. About such houses passersby are more likely to say, "Who on earth would want to live with such a color?"

How to Buy Color

It's time to talk about practical matters. The philosophers may describe color in terms of radiant energy, but how do you describe that to a clerk in a paint store? How do you buy everything you need connected to that color? Sheets? Towels? Wallpaper? Fabric? If you are your own decorator, you need to know how to go about finding the color you want to live with so that it won't disappoint you later or cost you more than it should.

Buying color means a lot of legwork. It means going to paint stores and looking at color charts. It means going through those mountains of big books in the wallpaper department. It means going to carpet stores to get ideas for walls and slipcover colors. It means examining the colors of an Oriental or a dhurrie rug to look for connections with other color choices. It means investigating all the new kinds of colors that are available in flooring materials. It means going to bed-linen departments and roaming the display areas. The colors of cotton terry towels are an excellent source of color inspiration. Just looking at a few different-colored towels stacked together might put together a bathroom scheme for you.

The color shopper also goes to the china department and looks at the colors in tableware and to stores that sell quality Oriental case goods and to the venetian blind store to match a wall or rug color. As you look, you can collect samples. Memorizing color is not the same as memorizing a telephone number or a tune. It's virtually impossible even for someone like me who deals with color all the time to retain a shade and put it together with another shade in my mind. If you don't have an actual sample of a color, don't use it.

If you're working with sheeting as fabric, make sure that you buy enough. As vast as the selection of sheets is, it is also ephemeral. Patterns come and go, and only the ones that sell stay on and on. Buy more than you think you will need, and you will have enough to line the draperies.

Keep a folder for your house as you select samples for your color palette where your little bits of fabric and carpet and color sticks can be kept together. Taking notes is also a good idea.

What to Do About Color Trends

Color trends come and go. Remember the 1950s when there was pink and gray everything? Typically the look was pink walls, gray carpet, gray sofa, and pink-and-white accent pillows. Today's grayed-out, postmodern colors aren't that far from the fifties look, so if you had held out against changing your living room decor for thirty years, you would be back in fashion again! At the moment, I would guess that the postmodern look will last about as long as the pink-and-gray 1950s look lasted.

I get calls and letters all the time regarding color trends. What are the current "in" colors? What's on the "out" list? I never think of colors as "in" or "out," but rather what colors are to each other in combination. I remember some years ago a fashion editor of a major magazine took a trip to India. Soon all the models in her magazine were wearing red dots painted in the middle of their foreheads. Then she began to embellish, and her models appeared with red dots in their navels and stars and half-moons in various colors pasted all over their bodies. It didn't quite make it as a fashion look. Home decoration can be the same way: if you try to put together disconnected parts of a faraway chic and make it work in your hometown, you may never be quite satisfied with the final results.

One current trend that's here to stay, though, is Chinese, which is more popular than ever and deservedly so. The way the Chinese live has always had much appeal for the rest of the world, ever since the days of Marco Polo. It makes sense that the Chinese influence has begun to play an important color role in decorative tastes, especially in regard to color. As we all know, anything Chinese is going to be colorful, and many people have been afraid of color. However, I'm beginning to see more jade-colored walls and black lacquer with gold than ever before, and as a color lover, this pleases me.

Buying Color in Paint

As we all know, painters love north light and they love to paint on a cloudy day. Why? Because light stabilizes on a cloudy day. It is not constantly shifting. Imagine trying to paint a face, and every time you look up the angle of the shadow has changed ever so slightly as has the flesh tone. What light does to color and the effort to duplicate that effect are what painters spend a lifetime studying. The interplay of light and color is also what makes buying color such a tricky business. What you see in the paint store is only half the story. What happens when you get that paint home and smear it on the wall is the whole story.

Anyone who has bought a package of dye at the five-and-dime knows how fraught with disappointment the dyeing process can be. The same thing is true at the paint store. People order what they want by number and the paint mixer is asked to mix up a gallon of B-183, which he does by adding pigment in powdered form according to the formula. It's supposedly all very accurate and scientific, but it's really a rather miraculous process.

Now you have to take that gallon home and see how its color looks in the light. But people usually buy color during the day. What they bought may be a perfect day color, but what about night? What does the incandescent bulb do for it? Anything? Both daylight and night light have to flatter your color. I always suggest painting a complete wall, with the contrasting trim color, before painting the whole room. Even then, you won't get the full impact before painting the whole room.

Remember that paint dries a different color from the one in the paint can. If you have just bought a burgundy red, remember that dark colors dry lighter on the wall and light colors dry darker. I always recommend that people use washable oil-based paints. With an oil base, even in a flat finish, you can wash the walls. This is especially important in the darker colors. If you paint your walls a dark green in a water-based paint and put a piece of furniture against the wall, you've got an abrasion with the first bump of that piece against the wall. This abrasion won't happen with the more durable oil-based finish. I like to use a flat finish on the wall itself and a semigloss for the trim.

In the morning, you can check the way the room color reflects morning light. You should do this again at noon and at mid-afternoon. This is a weekend task, when you can be home for a twenty-four-hour period. If your color is too light or too dark, you take the gallon back to the paint store and talk about an adjustment with the paint-store clerk. As does a custom-tailored garment, custom-mixed paint needs a fitting. You and your color taste should be satisfied.

Another element in the adjustment of paint color is the nature of the surface of your wall. Surface has a great deal to do with the look of the finished painted wall. Drywall, masonry, plastic, and wood all have different absorbing qualities, which affect color.

Buying Color in Wall Coverings

When you work with wallpaper, you don't have to worry about so many light variables as you do when you work with paint. What you see is pretty much what you get, and results vary little. The color of wallpaper is also more stable than paint. It fades less as the years go by. I like to use solid-color wall coverings, or those with a subtle texture to them like a *strié* (which is a vertical stripe of a color close in tone to the background), a tweed, a marbleized texture, or a gemlike pattern that looks like jade, jasper, or malachite. There are a lot of interesting solid-color wall treatments in wall coverings of paper, silk, linen, grass cloth, and other fibers.

Buying wall covering is also good for thinking about common denominators in your color decorating. Over the years I've come to believe that the best common denominator is the stripe. Stripes work with geometrics, florals, solid colors, and all styles. I particularly like to use a stripe in a low-ceilinged room because the vertical lines give the room a feeling of height. If you use a stripe of soft yellow and apple green in a room with a seven-foot-high ceiling, it will give that room a feeling of another foot or two. You can paint that ceiling yellow and use a yellow, green, and pink floral print for the curtains or upholstery.

Buying Color in Patterns

I always design a wallpaper or fabric pattern with a sense of knowing what it's going with. I can't choose a pattern in isolation. Unfortunately, when most designers decide on patterns, they often do so without reference to anything else. But I believe that when you buy sheets, for instance, you should know what the colors are going to be that will be living with them. What color are the walls? If you have brown walls, you might look at a sheet pattern with a teal background with brown branches and blue and melon flowers. When I design wallpaper or fabric patterns, I always create three or four color schemes in my head that my patterns will work with. When you buy a sheet pattern, think of the kinds of color schemes you could use that sheet pattern with, so that if you were to decide to change your walls to beige or your carpet to melon or alabaster, your sheets would still coordinate with your decor. Try to buy colors that are versatile.

Ideally, a pattern should be one that can serve in all rooms of the house—kitchen, dining room, living room, bedroom, or family room. If it has this versatility, then it's a classic pattern. When you look at a sheet pattern, ask yourself if you would want to use it in the living room. If so, go ahead and buy it.

The same universality of design should apply to kitchen patterns. Why does kitchen fabric have to have food in it? Why does a boy's wallpaper have to have soldiers on it? The answer is simple: it doesn't. I would stay away from those "special interest" designs and would pass by the books in the wall-covering department that have titles like "Patterns for Kitchens" or "Patterns for Your Bathroom," where the silvery patterned paper is sure to feature swans on a lily pad.

I try to aim for "Patterns for Everywhere." If I want a strawberry in a pattern, that strawberry should be entwined with the little white strawberry flowers. I could design such a pattern on a blue ground and tie it with a bow. Then I could make it work in the kitchen, a bedroom, a dining room, and even a living room if the scale of the pattern were large enough. I could make that strawberry wall covering work in every room of the house, including the hallways. By not designing the strawberry in its full fruit, thereby limiting it to the kitchen, I can use the strawberry motif throughout a home.

Can you imagine, for instance, using a strawberry wallpaper in the bathroom? It just wouldn't work. It would make people think of strawberries floating in the bathtub. However, strawberry flowers would work well in that room. People don't want to think about food in the bathroom, but people do like to see grass, clouds, or geometrics there.

An exception to the rule of no food in the bathroom and rarely in the bedroom is the Chinese pomegranate. It is so versatile that it will work anywhere. I like to use pomegranate trees in wallpaper design. It's a very welcoming pattern. It looks especially good in an entryway in a combination of pomegranate, aqua blue, greens, peach, and red on an ecru-colored ground.

Over the years I've found that people like trees and vines in their wallpapers and choose them in all sorts of colors. It's a good choice. On a ground of sky blue, peach, pink, or ecru, the wallpaper colors can be connected well through an entire house.

Buying Colors in Combination

I suggest that as you shop for color you collect color samples for everything. Ask a sales clerk for a bit of the brilliant blue-green or peacock-blue fabric that you are considering and put it together with other colors that are in the running for your color beauty contest. I always suggest that you put all the colors together before you buy any one of them. The high cost of carpeting alone allows for no whims or mistakes in that purchase. Remember to consider the versatility factor in carpeting. Say you wanted to change the color of your draperies or walls a few years from now. Could you? Or are you locked into too few color choices by your carpet? Remember that you don't have to change the carpet and wall color at the same time.

Another important aspect to buying color is remembering the color tastes of those you buy for. Your youngest child is not the same color person as your grown-up son or your elderly mother. A young person can live with wild, shocking colors and not be overly stimulated by them. But rare is the person in his fifties or sixties who is able to do so. The older person wants stimulation that is less abrasive. I believe it is changes in the eye that make people deviate from their long-held color choices over the decades. In the case of Ethel Merman, her choices went from bright, bright red to the more subdued mauves, deep greens, and beiges. Rare is the elderly person who dresses in primary colors. Given a choice elderly people don't want to live with them either. Conversely it is the rare child who wants to live with sophisticated colors.

Buying Color in Accessories

Accessories are really the key to outstanding decorating with color in your rooms: the paintings, the scrolls, the hardware on the doors, the potted flower, the china, the enamels and glazes on your pottery, your pieces of colored glass or gemstones.

These are the color objects that attract the eye and these are the things that people tend to think of last or sometimes not at all, which makes for sterility and conformity in their homes. These people think that what is important are the things they sit on, write on, or dine on. These things are important, of course, but they can't carry a room. What carries a room and makes it work are accessories. They really say who you are.

Color in your rooms is there to enhance the color of your accessories. Maybe what you value most are your paintings and photographs. What color walls would enhance them best? Lately I have seen a drastic change in the colors that museums use for the display of paintings. Once a museum had to have white walls and that was that. Yet, if you look at the walls of the great palaces and homes of Italy, France, and the Far Eastern cultures, you will never see such a sterile approach. Museum directors and art gallery owners around the world have begun to show their collections against background colors of gray, burgundy, dark blue, and even black. Why? Because they provide a color mood. When you think about Tintoretto, you might choose a background of gray with gold trim on the ceiling. Add burgundy chairs and you have a Tintoretto setting.

I often recommend working from a painting for a color scheme, or from a multicolored piece of china or pottery that you love. Ask yourself just what it is that you love about it. Maybe you own a landscape with a blue sky, white mountains, green fir trees, and a log cabin with a man in the front yard dressed in a red and black mackinaw jacket and green knickers. You can take the colors in that single painting and make them your master color plan. You could paint the walls a sky blue and the trim cloud white. You could get a carpet the color of the fir trees and choose dark wood furniture in walnut, teak, and mahogany. Then you could find a country check in a red and black plaid and put it on the sofa, and cover a pair of chairs in the color of the man's knickers. There are ways of doing entire rooms and even entire homes around important accessories.

Perhaps you would like to take your inspiration from a valuable and beloved piece of china such as Crown Derby, which is blue, rust, gold, and white. You could do a Crown Derby room with a deep indigo blue carpet, rust walls, lots of brass lamps and accessories, a fabric of rust, blue, and beige for the sofa, and pull-up chairs upholstered in rust.

A Final Reminder

Remember that when buying color you are thinking not just of your response to that color alone but what it looks like in combination with other colors. Above all, colors have to treat each other in a positive way. Like a group of friends, they all have to get along or there will be trouble in the air. If you are thinking of introducing a new color you have just met and are all excited about, take a sample of it to your house and see how it gets along with the colors you already live with. I love color, and believe there should be more of it in the world, but I'm also a color traditionalist. That approach has made my involvement with color one of continuing enjoyment.

Index

adolescents:
  bedroom for, 153
  color choices of, 45–46
advertising, 46–48
airplane interiors, 60
alchemy, 88, 90
Americana style, 102–105
  color wheel of, 102–103
  Victorian, 110–12
  regional, 107–108
American Colonial style, 105–107, 131
  boy's room in, 151–52
  color wheel of, 105–106
  exterior colors in, 159
American-modern style, 119–21
  bedrooms in, 120–21, 154–55
  color wheel of, 119–20
aniline dyes, 110–11
appetite-stimulating colors:
  in dining room, 48–49, 138–40
  in kitchen, 143, 144

Architectural Digest, 29
architectural furnishings, 52
Art Deco style, 23, 28, 134
 postmodern style and, 115,
  118, 119
 black-loving people and, 28
arzica, 91
autumn people, 62, 64–67,
 69–70, 158
avocado, 14–16, 50
azurite, 90, 92, 93

baby's room, 149–50
Ballet Russe, 112
Barclay Hotel (London), 19
bathroom(s), 156–59
 black, 28–30
 for blue-lovers, 7–8
 choosing patterns, 168
 cosmetic seasons and,
  157–58
 raspberry, 158–59
 for yellow-lovers, 10
bedroom(s), 147–56
 adolescent's, 153
 in American-modern style,
  120–21, 154–55
 architectural approach to
  color choice in, 52
 black, 29
 blue-lovers and, 7
 brown in, 35
 children's, 149–53, 167
 color connectives and,
  126–27
 color coordination in, 154
 infant's, 149–50
 pastel/melon, 155
 for red-loving people, 3
 for spring person, 68
 white, 33–34
 for winter person, 67
 yellow, 9–10, 155–56

beige, 14, 36, 37
 as conservative color, 125
 in postmodern style, 115,
  116
Bermuda, 110, 160
Bible, 84–85
bitter-tasting colors, 47–48
black, 26–30
 combinations with, 56
 history of use of, 92
 lovers of, 26–29
 meanings of, 26, 45, 100
 Oriental use of, 28
 and winter people, 65, 157
bloodstone, 89
blue, 6–9
 in Americana style, 104
 children and, 43
 combinations with, 55–56
 and dining room, 142
 as enhancer of other colors,
  46–47
 and four seasons, 62–64
 history of use of, 83–85, 87,
  89–91
 as male color, 151
 meanings of, 6, 45, 100
 as neutral color, 37–40
 personality of lovers of, 6–7
 physiological effects of, 44
 varieties of, 8
blue green, 16–17
boats, 6
bodily responses, *see*
  physiological effects of
  color
boy's bedroom, 151–52, 167
brazilwood, 101
brown, 34–36
 in Americana style, 105
 as appetite stimulator, 138,
  139
 history of use of, 83, 92–93

meaning of, 34, 45
men vs. women and, 34–35
buying color, 162–71
   accessories as guide to,
      169–71
   color trends and, 163–64
   combining samples prior to,
      168–69
   paint, 164–66
   taste differences and, 169
   wall coverings, 166
   wallpaper/fabric patterns,
      167–68

cadmium, 88
California style, 108
   See also Southern California;
      Southwestern style
Caribbean, 72, 73, 109–110
casinos, 59–60
cave paintings, 84
celadon, 18
celadonware, 100
ceiling height, living-room,
   132
Cennini, Cennino d'Andrea,
   88–89, 91
changing colors, 75–79, 94
chemical vs. natural colors, 82,
   86, 88, 89, 93–94, 103
Chicago, 107
children, 169
   bedrooms for, 15, 149–53
   color and psychology of,
      42–44, 46, 149
   and purple, 19
China, *see* Oriental style
Christmas colors, 56, 57,
   59–60, 133
cinnabar, 85–86
cloisonné enamel colors,
   100
closure, principle of, 128

Colonial style, *see* American
   Colonial style
color combinations, 55–57
color connection/coordination,
   124–28
   in conservative house,
      125–27
   three principles of, 127–28
color consultants, 64
color illusion, 51–55
   figure on ground, 53–55
   reduction of bulk, 51–53
color-preference tests, 50–51
coloring materials, history of,
   82–94
complexion, type of, *see*
   cosmetic colors
connectives, *see* color
   connection/coordination
Continental style:
   blue lovers and, 7
   celadon and, 18
   English style as part of, 94
   white and, 30–31, 33
   yellow-lovers and, 10
   see also English style; French
      style; Italian style
continuity, principle of, 127–28
coordination, *see* color
   connection/coordination
copper blue, 90–91
cosmetic colors, 62–70
   autumn, 62, 64–67, 69–70,
      158
   and bathroom, 157–58
   how to determine, 64
   spring, 62–66, 68, 157
   summer, 62–66, 68–69,
      157–58
   winter, 62–67, 133, 157
Craftsman's Handbook, The
   (Cennini), 88–89
Crawford, Joan, 5, 31–32, 157

denim, 87
Depression colors, 112–13
dining room(s), 138–43
   appetite-stimulating colors
      for, 48–49, 138–40
   blue-lovers and, 7
   color connectives and, 126
   lighting of, 141
   mint green, for summer
      person, 69
   open to kitchen/living
      room, 142–43
   Oriental-style, 142, 143
   postmodern colors in, 141
   for red-loving people, 3
   for yellow-lovers, 9–12
Dior, Christian, 97
Draper, Dorothy, 13, 19–20,
      115, 135
drawing room, English-style,
      95–96
dyes, 83, 84, 88, 102
   Americana style and,
      102–103
   aniline, 110–11
   Oriental, 100–101

Easter colors, 56–57
elder leaves, 84
Empire style, 3, 106
English style, 78, 94–96,
      131
   drawing room in, 95–96
   library in, 95
   living room in, 136–37
   purple in, 19
   ten colors of, 94–95
   use of green in, 17
Exodus, Book of, 84, 85
exterior colors, 159–60

family room, 146–47
figure on ground, 53–55

finger painting, 43
Florida, 73–74, 107–109
Fortuny fabrics, 99
Fourth of July colors, 56
French Empire style, 3, 106
French style, 10, 24, 39,
      96–98, 132
   color wheel of, 97
   pastels in, 38–39
   raspberry bathroom in,
      158–59
full-force-color rooms, 57–59

garden colors, 57–59
Gingold, Hermione, 21
girl's bedroom, 152–53
gold (color), four seasons and,
      66
gold (metal), 93
grass green, 17
gray, 36, 39
   in Americana style, 104
   with black, 27, 29
   blue with, 55–56
   meaning of, 45, 47
   in postmodern style, 29,
      115–18
green, 12–18
   in Americana style, 103
   as appetite stimulator, 138,
      139
   avocado, 14–16
   blue green, 16–17
   celadon, 18
   in English style, 95
   and four seasons, 64, 67
   grass (green-apple), 17
   history of use of, 84, 91, 92
   meaning of, 12–13, 45,
      59–60
   personality of lovers of,
      12–14
   red and, 56, 57, 59–60, 133

for shutters, 159, 160
in Victorian style, 112
and wood, 135
green yellow, 50

hall, 129–30
color connections and, 125
Harlow, Jean, 23, 30
Hawaii, 109
hematite, 83, 89
Homer, 85, 91–92
hotel rooms, 70–71

illusion, *see* color illusion
indigo, 84–85, 87, 90, 91, 101
Ireland, 71–72
island-living style, 72, 73,
    109–110
Italian style, 98–99
color wheel of, 98
dining room in, 99

Jefferson, Thomas, 38
Jensen, Georg, 69

kitchen(s), 143–46
appetite-stimulating colors
    in, 48–49, 143, 144
orange, 26
patterns in, 167
for red-lovers, 4–5
wood in, 145, 146

lacquer, 100, 101, 115
for red walls, 3–4, 77–78
lapis lazuli, 82, 86, 90, 93
lavender, 20–23
Leonardo da Vinci, 93
lilac, 21, 22
lime white, 92
living room(s), 131–37
in American-modern style,
    120

architectural approach to
    color choice in, 52–53
for autumn person, 69–70
brown, 36
ceiling height in, 132
in Colonial style, 106–107
color connectives and,
    125–27
English-style, 136–37
in fire orange, 24–25
light in, 131
mood of, 132–34
in Oriental style, 101–
    102
postmodern, 119
for red-lovers, 3
in Southwestern style,
    135–36
for summer person, 68–69
white, 33
wood in, 134–35
local colors, 70–74
see also specific regions and styles

madder root, 84, 86, 101
Maine, 107–108
maintenance vs. redecoration,
    78–79
malachite, 92, 93
manganese, 83
Marimekko (designer), 32
mauve, 110
Mediterranean style,
    red-lovers and, 3, 4
men vs. women, color
    preferences of, 34–35,
    49–50
Merman, Ethel, 20, 169
minium, 91–92
modern style, *see*
    American-modern style
Mondrian colors, 117, 131,
    154

Monticello, 38, 105–106
murex, 88

natural vs. chemical colors, 82,
    86, 88, 89, 93–94, 103
neon, 114
neutral colors, 37–40
    see also pastels; *and specific colors*
New Orleans, 107
1940s style, 113–14
1950s style, 114, 120, 134, 163
1960s style, 114, 120–21
1970s style, 114

ochre, 83, 84, 89, 91
Odyssey (Homer), 85
O'Keeffe, Georgia, 135
one-color schemes, 40
orange, 23–26
    as appetite stimulator,
        138–39
    history of use of, 91
    meanings of, 45, 46, 48
    Thais and, 23–24, 91
    personality of lovers of, 24
Oregon, 107
Oriental style, 24, 78, 99–102,
    114–15, 131, 164
    and Americana style, 105
    in bedroom, 154
    black, 28
    color wheel of, 101
    dining room in, 142, 143
    as element of French style, 97
    orange in, 23–25, 91
    and spring person, 68
orpiment, 91

Pacific Northwest colors, 107
packaging, color in, 46–48
paint:
    how to buy, 164–65
    type of surface and choice
        of, 166

paintings as guide to color
    choices, 170–71
Palm Beach, 38, 108, 160
pastels, 38–40
    brown and, 35
    and color connections,
        127
    French, 38–39
    Palm Beach, 38
    social class and preference
        for, 45
    see also specific colors
patterns, choice of, 167–68
physiological effects of color,
    44–45
pigments, 83, 84, 88, 89
pink:
    exterior, 160
    in packaging, 46, 47
    psychological effects of, 45
    soft, 37, 39
plastic, advent of, 113–14
Pliny, 86
postmodern style, 82, 115–19,
    131, 141, 163
    bedroom in, 29–30
    color ranges in, 21–23
    color wheel of, 115, 116
    dining room in, 141
    for summer person, 68–69
powder room in black, 28
primary vs. secondary colors:
    age and, 169
    personality and, 12
psychedelic colors, 114
psychological reactions to
    color:
    appetite stimulation, 48–49,
        138–40, 143, 144
    in children, 19, 42–44, 46
    purple, 19
Puerto Rico, 109
Pump Boys and Dinettes
    (musical), 113

purple, 18–23
  blue with, 56
  general characteristics of,
    18–19
  history of use of, 83–85, 88
  meaning of, 19, 45
  as "old" color, 20–21
  postmodern, 20–23

radiators, 129
realgar yellow, 91
red, 2–5, 77–78
  in advertising, 46
  in Americana style, 104–105
  as appetite stimulator, 140
  children and, 43
  combinations with, 56
  and four seasons, 64, 65, 67
  green and, 56, 57, 59–60,
    133
  history of use of, 83–86, 89
  meanings of, 2, 45, 47, 60,
    100
  personality of lovers of, 2–5
  physiological effects of, 44
  primary, types of, 3
redecoration vs. maintenance,
    78–79
Renaissance style, 3, 98, 99
Ripamonti, Rosanna, 64
Ritz Hotel (Paris), 97
Rolls-Royce green, 95

saffron, 86–87, 91, 101
sage green, 92
Saint Laurent, Yves, 62, 131,
    133
St. Patrick's Day colors, 56
salty colors, 48
sap, 84, 100
scarlet, history of use of,
    84–86
schools, 117
seasons, *see* cosmetic colors

secondary vs. primary colors:
  age and, 169
  personality and, 12
Sequoia (presidential yacht), 6
shopping, *see* buying
showcase houses, 61
shutters, 159, 160
sienna, raw and burnt, 84
silk, 100
silver (color), winter person
    and, 65–67
silver (metal), 93
similarity, principle of, 127
Sinopia, 89
size of room, color and
    perception of, 78
slipcovers, 146–47
"smell" of colors, 48
Southern California, 107, 109
  see also Southwestern style
Southampton (Long Island),
    108
Southwestern style, 35–36,
    72–74, 107, 108
  living room in, 135–36
spring people, 62–66, 68, 157
stained glass, 83, 85
studio apartment, redecoration
    of, 76–78
summer people, 62–66, 68–69,
    157–58
sun-room, island-living-style,
    109

Taiwan, 114
terra rosa, 89
  dining room in, 99
terre verte, 92
tests for color preference,
    50–51
Thailand, 23–24, 91, 101
  see also Oriental style
Thanksgiving colors, 56
trim, 128–29

turmeric, 101
turquoise, 113–14

ultramarine, 82, 89–90
umber, 84, 105

verdigris green, 92
vermilion, 82, 85–86, 89,
   91–92
   as appetite stimulator, 138,
   140
Victorian style, 110–12
   lavender-lovers and, 22–
   23
violet, red with, 56
Virgin Islands, 109

wall coverings:
   how to buy, 166
   patterns of, 167–68
walnut shells, 101
"weight" of colors, 49
Western colors, 72
   see also Southwestern style
white, 30–34
   in Americana style, 104
   exterior, 159, 160
   and four seasons, 65
   history of use of, 92
   meaning of, 100
   personality of lovers of,
   30–32

White House, 125
white lead, 92
Williamsburg style, 105–
   107
   celadon with, 18
   and woodwork, 129
winter people, 62–67, 133,
   157
woad, 87
women vs. men, color
   preferences of, 34–35,
   49–50
wood(work), 128–29
   in kitchen, 145, 146
   in living room, 134–35
Wright, Frank Lloyd, 113

yellow, 9–12
   in Americana style, 103
   as appetite stimulator, 138,
   139
   combinations with, 56
   and four seasons, 64–66
   history of use of, 83, 84,
   86–88, 91
   meanings of, 9, 11, 45,
   100
   personality of lovers of,
   9–11
   soft, 37
"Your Family Decorator"
   (newspaper column), 14

CARLETON VARNEY is known to Americans as "Your Family Decorator"—the headline of his nationally syndicated column —and was also seen by millions on his syndicated television show "Inside Design." He has designed everything from matchbooks to skyscrapers, as well as projects like The Greenbrier Hotel, White Sulphur Springs, West Virginia; The Grand Hotel at Mackinac Island, Michigan; Dromoland Castle, Ireland; and M/S World Discoverer, Singapore. As a design consultant to the White House, Mr. Varney planned the decor for the Israel-Egypt Treaty Celebration, and is currently curator of the Presidential Yacht Trust, working on the refurbishing of the presidental yacht, *Sequoia*.

Chairman of the fabric and wallcovering firm of Carleton V. Ltd. and president of Dorothy Draper & Company, Inc., both of New York City, Mr. Varney also operates an English antiques and oriental arts business at White Sulphur Springs, West Virginia, known as Carleton Varney at The Greenbrier. He is dean of a college of interior design—the Carleton Varney School—at the University of Charleston, Charleston, West Virginia. Mr. Varney lives in New York City with his designer wife, Suzanne, and their three sons. *Color Magic* is his fourteenth book.